VICTORIN(

C000064285

SWISS ARMY KNIFE
WHITTLING
BOOK 43 EASY PROJECTS

Chris Lubkemann

FOX CHAPEL
PUBLISHING

ACQUISITION EDITOR: Alan Giagnocavo
DEVELOPMENTAL EDITOR: Mindy Kinsey
JUNIOR EDITOR: Carly Glasmyre
TECHNICAL EDITOR: Bob Duncan
COPY EDITOR: Katie Weeber
COVER & LAYOUT DESIGNER: Jason Deller
PHOTOGRAPHY: Scott Kriner

Other books by Chris Lubkemann:
The Little Book of Whittling
Big Book of Whittle Fun
Tree Craft
Whittling Twigs & Branches

Victorinox Swiss Army Knife Whittling Book was first published in 2015 by Fox Chapel Publishing Company, Inc.

ISBN 978-1-56523-877-0

To learn more about the other great books from Fox Chapel Publishing, or to find a retailer near you, call toll-free 800-457-9112 or visit us at *www.FoxChapelPublishing.com*.

Note to Authors: We are always looking for talented authors to write new books. Please send a brief letter describing your idea to Acquisition Editor, 1970 Broad Street, East Petersburg, PA 17520.

Printed in China
Second printing

Carl Elsener, Sr. (1922–2013)

Dedication

Although I never had the privilege of meeting Carl Elsener, Sr., I know that during the many years he spent leading the Victorinox Swiss Army family, he contributed immeasurably to what this outstanding company is today. For many decades, his passion for innovation and quality and his enthusiasm for the excellent product that consistently came out of the "Swiss Knife Valley" were evident.

I would like to dedicate this book to this very special man.

Chris Lubkemann
Lancaster, Pennsylvania

CONTENTS

PREFACE   7

INDEX   136

1 **GETTING STARTED** **10**
Choosing a Knife 12
Sharpening and Honing 16
Basic Cutting Strokes 18
Wood 20
Other Tools and Supplies 22

4 **BRANCH ANIMALS** **64**
The Ideal Wood Fork 65
Owl 66
Alligator 70
Horse Pen 74
Bird 78

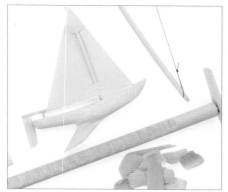

2 EASY UTENSILS & TOOLS . . 24
Knife. 26
Fork 35
Knitting Needles 40
Crochet Hook 42
Spoon. 45

3 TOYS **50**
Whimmy Diddle 52
Bow and Arrow 55
Sailboat .58

5 CURL CREATIONS **82**
The Ideal Knife Blade Bevel 83
Wet vs. Dry Wood 83
Carving Curls 84
Flower 86
Tree 89
Rooster. .92
Heron 106
Roadrunner 111
Squirrel. 118

6 SIMPLE BUT STUNNING . . . **126**
Table Art. 128
Utensil and Jewelry Trees 129
Simply Slices: Coasters, Checkers,
Necklaces, Tic Tac Toe, Magnets,
Napkin Rings. 130

Acknowledgments

Any book is the result of the contributions by many people. This one is certainly no different. First, Brian Huegel, an outstanding cutlery expert and the owner of Country Knives, Intercourse, Pa., helped me touch base with Carl Elsener, Jr., the CEO of Victorinox Swiss Army, the best-known knife company in the world. Carl Elsener, in turn, by his own enthusiastic interest and encouragement related to what could be done with a pocketknife, contributed immeasurably to the fulfillment of this project. Alan Giagnocavo, the owner and president of Fox Chapel Publishing, was willing to commit to the project and has given full support all along. Then the editorial staff, and particularly Mindy Kinsey, Fox Chapel's editor of magazines, has especially contributed, editing and fine-tuning the step-by-step directions and "map" of the book, helping to make it a clear, interesting, and fun presentation both to beginning whittlers (or carvers, if you prefer), as well as offering challenge to folks who have been carving for a long, long time. Scott Kriner, the very professional photographer, was great to work with, too. Thanks to ALL of you who were part of the *Victorinox Swiss Army Knife Whittling Book* team!

PREFACE

The son of missionary parents, I spent most of my first thirteen years in the rainforests of Brazil and Peru, surrounded by an amazing variety of trees and wood. I was always close to the chisels, knives, and other hand tools that my dad worked with. I remember making toys, boats, traps, slingshots... Even when I returned to the United States for school, I never lost my appreciation for wood.

In the summer of 1966, I was introduced to the forked-branch roosters whittled by Appalachian Mountain folk artists. Working with a pocketknife purchased at a country store and a few pointers from Dr. John Luke, I whittled my first branch rooster. It looked like it had gotten into a terrible fight... and lost!

Chris Lubkemann

But, at least it looked like a rooster, not a pigeon, duck, or ostrich! I kept at it, and that same pocketknife helped me pay for my senior year of college, and more after that.

Now, closing in on fifty years later, the branch whittling concept has broadened to include many other projects, using branches from dozens of species of trees and bushes, scraps of milled wood, and even popsicle sticks, chopsticks, and toothpicks! Thousands of people in many countries have joined the whittling fun. I have given programs and demonstrations in schools, civic clubs, camps, shopping malls, churches, television programs, and countless other venues. It has been extremely satisfying to see folks from nine to ninety pick up the pocketknife/whittling concept and run with it!

I've used a few knives since retiring that first one, but nearly twenty years ago, my pocketknife of choice became a Victorinox Tinker Swiss Army Knife someone had given to me. To make it easier to work with the small blade, I removed the key ring and its tab, and tapered the small blade to a finer point. And, *WOW! I discovered what a treasure I had!* Since then, my Victorinox Swiss Army Knife has been my go-to tool for thousands of pieces, and a number of other popular models have joined my knife family. I've recommended to countless people the knives that have served me so well both in my carving and in many situations in regular life. (More on those later.)

To demonstrate my style of whittling to Mr. Elsener, I modified a new Swiss Army Knife (see pages 12 and 83) and used it to carve a small pile of twigs and bark (top photo). I sent a good number of the finished pieces from this collection of branch animals, knives, flowers, trees, name logs, and other projects—along with the knife—to Switzerland (bottom photo). That was the beginning of this book!

Chris Lubkemann whittles wherever he is—even while waiting for dinner at a restaurant. And he uses his Swiss Army Knife for much more than whittling; here, he is repairing a fan.

My personal connection with Victorinox Swiss Army began in 2013, when I began corresponding with Carl Elsener, Jr., the company's CEO. To make a long, interesting story short, I sent a modified Hiker pocketknife to Mr. Elsener, along with a number of pieces I had whittled with it. As we corresponded about knives, the idea arose to create a book about whittling with a Swiss Army Knife. I most often use the Tinker and Hiker, but the projects in this book are applicable to *any* model that has the standard small and large blades. They are all sharp enough to begin working with directly out of the original package. Hence, this book is for *anyone* who owns, or will own, a Swiss Army Knife. (If you want to do my modifications, you can—see pages 12 and 13. They are especially useful if you want to do the mini-mini-miniatures!)

Naturally, in the photos throughout the book, I'm carving with my own knives. Here's hoping that you, too, will use your knife and apply what you find in the pages that follow to discover the pleasure and satisfaction of creating your own special pieces, and to add your own chapter to this very rich and rewarding story of whittling.

Enjoy your knife, and happy whittling!

Chris Lubkemann

This is one of my first roosters, carved in 1966.
They really do get better, and fast!

CHAPTER ONE

GETTING STARTED

Whether you are new to whittling or an experienced carver, it's always a good idea to start with the basics—or, if you are in the latter category, to at least review the basics. In the following pages I've described a few tips and techniques that I think will make your whittling easier and more enjoyable. We'll talk about choosing a knife, sharpening it, the basic cuts you'll make with it, the types of wood you'll use it on, and the other supplies you'll need to complete the projects in this book.

The most important rule for carving, and one I can't emphasize enough, is that your knife must be sharp—really sharp, not "sort of sharp"! It is definitely safer, easier, and more fun to carve with a truly sharp knife. Please take my word on it!

Choosing a Knife

I have been carving for almost fifty years. I started with an inexpensive pocketknife from the country store and have acquired dozens of different pocketknives since then. But for nearly twenty years, my main carving knife has been a Victorinox Tinker Swiss Army. (I use the Recruit and Hiker, too.)

There are several reasons I really appreciate, use, and recommend Swiss Army Knives. The models I use have at least two blades: a small blade that is 1"–1½" (25mm–38mm) long and a larger one that is 2"–2½" (51mm–61mm) long. (I use the small blade for the majority of my carving, but the larger one comes in handy, too.) I've found the stainless steel to be excellent; the blades sharpen well and hold an edge. These knives are built with a strong handle and tight connections between the handle and blades. And while the main working parts of my knives are the blades, I constantly use the other features—the awl, screwdrivers, saw (on the Hiker), and, after lunch, the toothpick! And, finally, these knives are available in many stores at a reasonable price for such high-quality and extremely useful pocketknives/multi-tools.

Modifications

I doubt that most people will end up carving as much as I have, and many of you will be happy to leave the knife just as it is and merely learn how to keep the blades "whittling sharp." However, if you do find yourself carving a lot, and especially if you want to make the really miniature pieces, there are two modifications I make to my knives. Both are simple and practical; one is related to comfort and the other to actual cutting:

1. Remove the key ring. If you're going to use the small blade a lot, the way you will in carving, the key ring will get in your way. Remove the ring and saw off the little tab that holds it, and then file off any sharp edges.

2. **Taper the blade's point.** A thinner point is better for carving tight turns. Use a sharpening stone to (gently!) taper the top and bottom of the small blade to a thinner point. Then, follow my instructions on pages 16 and 17 to resharpen and hone the blade.

LEFT: A new Tinker, fresh from the box.

RIGHT: My Tinker, modified for carving. Note the difference in the shapes of the blades.

 There are more than 100 styles of Victorinox Swiss Army Knives. All of them have a lifetime warranty against defects in materials and workmanship.

Swiss Army Knives for Carving

TINKER

Carving features:
- 3½" (89mm) handle
- Small knife blade
- Large knife blade
- Reamer/punch

Other useful tools:
- Phillips screwdriver
- Large screwdriver
- Small screwdriver
- Bottle opener
- Tweezers
- Can opener
- Wire stripper
- Plastic toothpick

HIKER

Carving features:
- 3½" (89mm) handle
- Small knife blade
- Large knife blade
- Reamer/punch
- Wood saw

Other useful tools:
- Phillips screwdriver
- Large screwdriver
- Small screwdriver
- Bottle opener
- Tweezers
- Can opener
- Wire stripper
- Plastic toothpick

RECRUIT

Carving features:
- 3¼" (8.3mm) handle
- Small knife blade
- Large knife blade

Other useful tools:
- Large screwdriver
- Small screwdriver
- Bottle opener
- Tweezers
- Can opener
- Wire stripper
- Plastic toothpick

A NOTE ABOUT THE SMALLEST KNIVES

Some knives, such as those in the Classic series, are terrific for carrying in your pocket or on your key chain, but the 2¼" (57mm)-long handle is pretty small for carving. Save these for light duty and use a larger knife for carving.

Sharpening and Honing

The first and most important rule of carving is that *your knife must be sharp*. The Victorinox Swiss Army Knives are among the few pocketknives that I've found to be sharp enough right out of the box to do decent carving. However, as with any good-quality knife, you will need to know how to sharpen and hone the blades in order to do the most precise and detailed carving.

There are all kinds of methods and devices for sharpening knives. I will share with you my own very simple sharpening system, but feel free to experiment and find what works best for you. Like any method or system, mine takes a little practice, but it does work, and I've been satisfied with it for quite a few years. The price is pretty good, too—practically nothing, after a very small initial investment.

If I'm starting out with a totally dull knife, or even a new one that's not sharp, I use a two-sided sharpening stone to start the process (see Step 1). Then, follow Steps 2–4 to hone, polish, and strop the blade so it's ready to carve. If I'm starting with a blade that only needs a touch of sharpening, I'll start with the finest grit of wet-or-dry sandpaper (Step 3) and finish with a few strops on the leather. Either way, be sure to wash your hands after sharpening and honing your knife. The gray residue on your hands will end up smudging your carving project.

SHARPENING TOOLS
(left to right): Two double-sided sharpening stones; wet-or-dry sandpaper in 320, 400, and 600 grits; block for the sandpaper; and leather strop with stropping compound. One stone is sufficient; I just happen to have two and both snuck into the photo.

1 With the blade not quite flat, move it across the coarse side of the stone using a circular motion. Then, make a few slicing motions across the stone. Don't lift or turn the blade as it goes across the stone. Flip the stone to the finer side and repeat.

2 Place wet-or-dry sandpaper on top of a block of wood, and repeat the sharpening motions you used in Step 1. Be sure to turn the blade over to get both sides.

3 Go through the grits from coarser (lower numbers) to finer (higher numbers). Even if your pieces of sandpaper are virtually smooth, they'll still work to polish the edge of the blade. I have used some of my little beat-up sheets for ten years and they are still working!

4 Finally, strop (wipe) the blade on a piece of leather. The rough backside of an old leather belt works fine. Apply a little bit of stropping compound to the strop. With the blade flat against the strop, stroke it away from the edge a few times on each side. Wipe the blade clean, and you're ready to carve.

 Victorinox Swiss Army Knives have a lifetime warranty against defects in material and workmanship.

Basic Cutting Strokes

There are many ways to cut with a knife. These are the strokes I use the most often. I am demonstrating them for right-handed carvers. Left-handers, of course, will reverse the hands, following a mirror image of the photographs.

Safety

I have been carving for many years and rarely, if ever, cut myself, largely because I constantly keep in mind a three-word rule: "Air, not meat!" The knife blade doesn't know the difference between wood (what you're carving) and meat (any part of you). So when you hold the wood and cut it, position your hands (and other parts) so the blade hits air on its follow-through, not meat. You won't believe how much this simple rule helps!

Next, make small, controlled cuts. Don't be too aggressive when you cut into the wood. And finally, keep your knife sharp! A sharp knife is much easier to control because you won't have to shove or tug it through the wood, and it won't have the tendency to skid as you're cutting.

Some carving instructors recommend that beginning carvers wear protective gear while they get used to their knife. They suggest an inexpensive gardening glove and a leather thumb guard (or even a piece of duct tape wrapped around your thumb). I don't like to have anything on my hand or fingers (and I always remember my three-word rule!), but I feel I should pass on these suggestions.

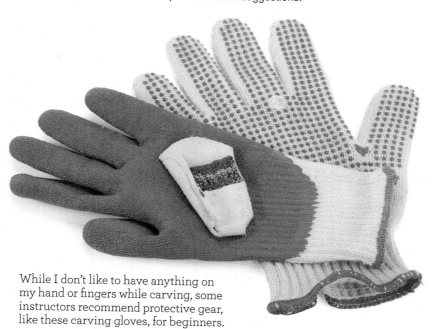

While I don't like to have anything on my hand or fingers while carving, some instructors recommend protective gear, like these carving gloves, for beginners.

Straightaway Cutting. This cut is good for removing a lot of wood or bark quickly. Hold the wood in your left hand and, using long, firm strokes, cut away from yourself with your right hand. Lock your right wrist so it doesn't bend during the cutting stroke. Don't dig too deeply into the wood on these strokes. You'll find it easier to make shallower strokes, even if it takes a few more slices to remove the same amount of wood.

Drawcutting. Hold the wood in your left hand and the knife in your right. Cut toward yourself (sort of like peeling an orange) with short strokes, using your right thumb as a brace against the wood. Keep your right thumb braced on your left thumb, not on top of the wood itself. That way, you don't run the risk of the blade cutting into your right thumb when it clears the end of the wood.

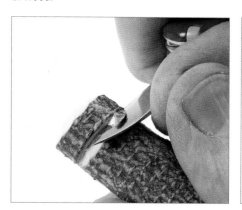

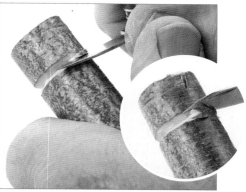

Thumbpushing. This particular stroke is practical for small cuts where you need precise control and don't want to overcut. Hold the wood in the four fingers of your left hand, leaving your left thumb free. Grip the knife in your right hand, keeping your right thumb against the back of the blade. With your left thumb, push either the back of the blade or the back of your right thumb.

V-notch. A combination of strokes, the V-notch is an extremely common and useful cut. Hold the knife at an angle toward the center of the cut and thumbpush into the wood. Turn either the knife or the project and make a second cut that meets the first in the bottom of the V; the chip should pop right out. Make a series of connected V-notches to cut a groove.

Wood

Assorted Blanks

Twigs and branches of all sizes are the main raw material I use for carving. They are abundantly available in my area, as well as in most of the world, I suspect—and they are usually free! I also enjoy carving bits of wood when I'm on vacation or teaching a class in a new area. I've had the fun of whittling wood in many countries of Europe and all over the United States, Canada, and Mexico, and have even worked on some great wood in Japan and the Philippines.

I definitely don't mean to imply that only branches will work for these projects. If you don't have immediate access to any good branches but do have a supply of straight-grained milled wood scraps, go ahead and experiment with what you have. I have also carved dowels, chopsticks, tongue depressors, craft sticks, and even toothpicks!

Characteristics of Good Branches

I'm guessing that I have carved more than eighty varieties of wood, the majority of them hardwoods. Some of my favorites include birch (any kind), maple, cherry, holly, beech, certain oaks, citrus wood, myrtle, olive, zambujeiro and lentisco (Portugal), alnos (Philippines), and guava. Because most of the branches I carve are relatively small and on the greenish side, the hardness of the wood hasn't been a problem.

More important than the variety are the characteristics of the branch in your hand. Even if you don't have the slightest idea of what species the wood is, see if it passes these four tests:

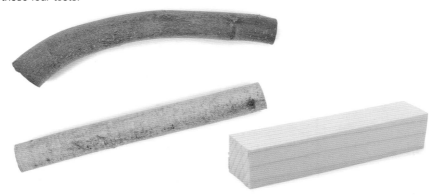

Straight grain: Most of the projects in this book call for straight-grained wood without a bunch of knots. If you find a curved branch, no problem; carve a beautiful letter opener with a curved blade.

Small pith   Large pith

Small pith: The spongy part in the center of a branch should be small, as shown above left. For instance, a ½" (13mm)-diameter branch should have a pith that is ¹⁄₁₆" (2mm) in diameter or smaller. A large pith (above right) will crumble when carved.

No sticky sap: This is one reason I avoid fresh pine. If I carved it, I'd be spending a lot of time cleaning sap off of my knife and hands. However, I often use kiln-dried, milled pine to make letter openers and plaques.

Fairly fresh: Because I work mainly with hardwoods, I prefer to carve wood that has some moisture in it. Some wood, such as beech, oak, and some fruitwoods, are very hard and need to be worked while they're still quite fresh. Others, including most birches, carve nicely when they've dried a bit. To keep twigs and branches from drying out too much, especially during the warmest months of the year, I cut them up and store them in plastic bags in the freezer. They can last for years that way! When a branch has become too hard or dry, you can soak it in water for a day or two, but then you have to let it partially re-dry before you can carve it. Often, it's easier to look for a new branch.

Note: You can cut wood at any time of the year. Even winter is great because it's easy to spot the best-shaped branches, and most woodland critters, like snakes and ticks, are tucked away sleeping ... or whatever they do!

WASH YOUR BRANCHES

If your branches are covered in soot, dust, mold, fungus, or dirt, just wash the bark. I use a rag, brush or scrubber, and a bucket of water. No sense getting the outside dirt on the clean inside wood as you carve!

Other Tools and Supplies

Besides a good knife, there are a number of other tools and supplies you'll need to finish the projects in this book. Many of them you probably already have. I'll cover some of the tools I use, but feel free to customize the list based on your preferences.

Pencil and permanent markers: You will need a pencil for occasional drawing and marking. You can use permanent markers of various colors for coloring some of the small woodburned designs you'll make.

Sandpaper: Choose a number of different grits in the fine to very fine range. For sharpening and honing, I use automotive wet-or-dry sandpaper, which comes in much finer grits than regular sandpaper does.

A large, dark cloth: This could be an old tablecloth, a piece of fabric, or an old bath towel. Although we photographed the projects in this book against a white background, out in the real world, it's much easier to see what you're doing against a dark background. Most wood is light-colored inside, so it's much easier to see the details of the carving if I hold my projects against a dark-colored background. Plus, it's easier to clean your chips if you catch them in a towel! (I think my wife has swept up my chips only three or so times in forty-eight years—probably one of the reasons we get along so well and have lasted so long!)

Wood glue: Any good wood glue.

Cyanoacrylate (CA) glue: I like to seal some projects, especially those with curls (flowers, trees, fancy feathers, etc.), with CA glue, such as Super Glue®. The glue penetrates the wood to seal and harden the thin curls. It also allows me to use water-based paints on parts that would otherwise uncurl, such as flower petals.

Woodburner: This tool is one of my favorites for personalizing projects with names, dates, and designs; I use it constantly. If you're just getting started, a woodburner from the craft store will work fine, although it's worth paying a little more to get the kind with adjustable heat. If you find yourself doing a lot of woodburning, consider investing in a better-quality machine that gets hotter; they are easier to use. I've found I can do pretty much everything I want with a writing tip.

Oil or acrylic paints and paintbrushes: Oil paints won't uncurl petals on projects like flowers. Acrylics work well on curls if used in conjunction with CA glue, and they are much easier to clean up than oil paints. I use brushes ranging in size from #00 to #2. Good-quality paintbrushes last longer and do a better job than cheap ones, and they won't shed bristles onto your project.

Clear finish: Most projects don't call for any finish, but polyurethane or a clear acrylic spray are good choices when you want to protect a piece. Note: Especially in humid conditions, never apply a water-based product (polyurethane or acrylic) to a rooster tail or other fine curl; it will uncurl before your eyes! Either use an oil-based product or wait until you're in dry conditions and lightly spray on the clear acrylic.

Handsaw: It's absolutely amazing what the saw blade on the Swiss Army Hiker will cut. I once used it to cut the entire length of an 8' sheet of masonite! However, if you're cutting a thick board or branch, you'll find a small handsaw useful. I also enjoy the Japanese pull saw, which is particularly useful for making the little slices for checkers, magnets, knitting needles, etc.

Rotary tool or other woodcarving tools: If you have access to rotary tools, chisels, drills, or other woodworking tools, feel free to use them. But, with the exception of some drilled holes and a few saw cuts, I carved all of the projects in this book with just my pocketknife.

 The Victorinox factory does not waste steel. After cutting the knife blades, Victorinox gives the leftover steel back to the supplier for new production. The company returns the steel filings produced during the grinding and polishing processes by reclaiming the steel and pressing it into cubes.

CHAPTER TWO

EASY UTENSILS & TOOLS

Whittling is an enjoyable pastime that you can do pretty much anywhere. You wouldn't believe all of the places and venues where I have carved! It is also a useful skill. From sharpening sticks for toasting marshmallows, to making a quick spoon for eating ice cream or yogurt, or a spreader to put mustard on a sandwich, as long as you have a stick and your pocketknife, you're not that many cuts away from the comforts of home.

I usually put a finish on my knives and letter openers, but I leave if off utensils that will touch food, like spoons and forks. If you prefer to add finish for home use, I suggest you use salad bowl finish. It's all natural, but let it dry for 24 hours before you use the tool or utensil.

Although you can start with any project in the book, they are organized roughly in order of difficulty, and some later projects build on skills and techniques learned in earlier chapters. I'm starting with the knife/letter opener because I've found that it's a good project for teaching basic cuts, and also is a very satisfying one to complete.

The techniques are basically the same for any size, whether it's a miniature piece or a very large one. In the following instructions I will note the size of the wood I'm using for the demonstration, but you feel free to change that to suit you. I frequently have fun making mini-mini projects from 1/16" (2mm)-diameter branches and even toothpicks!

FOR ALL THE PROS OUT THERE

If you are an experienced carver, you can take many of the basic projects and make them much more challenging. Try decorating the handles with carved patterns or designs, or experimenting with size. Add detail.

25

KNIFE

The knife is a great project to start with; it will get you familiar with your pocketknife and the basic cutting strokes. Knives of all sizes and shapes have been some of my favorite spontaneous whittling projects wherever I happen to be with my pocketknife and I find a piece of wood lying around, whether it's a small, straight twig, a foot-long branch, a scrap cut-off from a construction job, a tongue depressor, or even a toothpick (new or used). Naturally, the size of the knife will depend on the piece of wood you start with. Half of a little round toothpick will make for a perfect Bowie knife for Polly Pocket™! (Don't throw away the other half! It can turn into a flower, complete with petals, stem, and leaves. Instructions coming later.)

While a knife carved from wood will certainly not serve for all uses that a steel knife does, it still can be very useful, especially as a letter opener. And it definitely can be carved and finished in such a way that it becomes a beautiful piece of art. (That will be a fun challenge for all you carvers who already have lots of experience.)

The basic techniques are essentially the same for any size knife, whether it's one inch long or two feet long. The two basic parts of the knife will be (1) the handle and (2) the blade. As is the case with all knives, there can be a tremendous variety of shapes, designs, and styles, both on the handles as well as on the blades. Sometimes the shape and style will be partly dictated by the shape of the particular "blank" piece of wood you start out with.

MATERIALS

- Knife (Remember, sharp!)
- Smooth, straight-grained wood: ⅝"–¾" (16mm–19mm) dia. x 8"–9" (203mm–229mm) long
- Pencil
- Sandpaper: a couple of grits on the fine to very fine side (150- and 220-grit would work). Well-worn pieces of sandpaper are great for super-smooth fine-tuning!
- Cyanoacrylate (CA) glue, such as Super Glue®
- Woodburner with writing tip (optional)
- Clear finish, such as polyurethane

1 Choose a relatively smooth branch (as few knots as possible) with a small pith. If you're using a scrap of lumber, make sure it's straight-grained. Use a push cut to round the top of the branch all the way around to form the butt of the handle.

2 I like to carve a little grooved ring of V-notches at both ends of the handle. If you want to get creative, take advantage of the contrast between the darker bark and the lighter wood underneath and carve swirls, crosshatching, or other patterns on the handle.

4 (Optional) Sight down the stick end to end to plan the blade; turn the stick until the blade will be straight. Mark the sides of the blade. Then, use a series of long, even strokes to shave a swatch out of one or both sides of the handle. Cut toward the center of the swatch from both ends so that the cuts meet in the middle. Don't try to carve the whole swatch from one direction.

3 Decide how long you want the handle and blade to be. Carve a second grooved ring at the blade end of the handle.

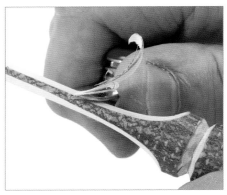

5 Use long, straight strokes to flatten both sides of the blade. I get a good long stroke by locking my wrist and pushing the knife all the way to the end of the branch. Take thin slices so you don't overcut, and stop before you get into the pith in the center of the branch.

6 Start the cut at the same point on the second side, and cut an even amount off both sides so the blade is centered on the handle.

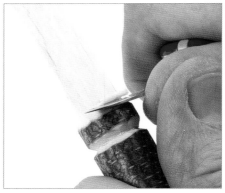

7 Remove the remaining little strips of bark from the top and bottom of the blade.

8 Make a fairly wide V-cut at the base of the blade where it joins the handle. Use your left thumb push on your right thumb as you make the cuts around the junction. Don't make the cuts too deep or you will weaken the blade/handle junction. You want the knife to be strong enough to be truly functional.

 All Swiss Army Knives are made in Switzerland of first-class stainless steel.

9 Sketch the blade shape you'd like your knife to have.

10 Use long strokes to remove wood on both sides of the point, following your pencil lines.

 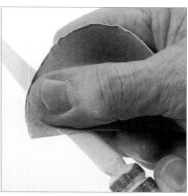

11 Sharpen the point and the blade edge. If the branch you're using is still fairly fresh, don't sharpen the edge too much. Let the wood dry a bit and firm up before you do your finer sharpening. When forming the point of the blade, especially if the pith is not extremely small, cut in such a way that the cutting edge of the point and the point itself are a bit off center. You don't want the cutting edge or point to be centered on the pith. You want the point of the knife and the entire cutting edge to be solid wood.

12 Once the wood has dried enough to allow for sanding, smooth the blade with fine sandpaper. If you take a little time, you can really fine-tune and sharpen the blade. Smooth the handle swatch, too.

13 Run cyanoacrylate (CA) glue along the edge and on the point to harden them. When the CA glue hardens, resand the edge and point to the sharpness you want. At this point, the basic knife is complete, but you can certainly customize it more if you want.

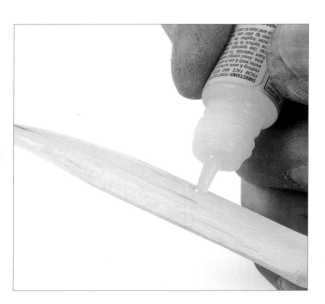

14 (Optional) I like to woodburn a name on one side of the handle and a scene on the other. Permanent markers work well for adding color. The possibilities are almost endless!

 Clean, sharpen, and oil your Swiss Army Knife regularly. Use a multi-purpose oil that is neutral in odor and taste, resistant to aging, has good wear and corrosion protection qualities, and is suitable for use with foodstuff. Clean your knife with warm water; never put it in the dishwasher.

15 After I complete a knife, I always put some kind of finish on it. The finish keeps the knife cleaner when you use it. Any polyurethane or clear acrylic will work; polyurethane finishes are harder, but acrylics dry faster.

Add challenge to the knife project by varying the size and handle or blade design.

SPREADER

The spreader has a thicker, more rounded blade than the knife. It can be used for jam, nut butters, mustard, and the like. To make one, follow the instructions for the knife through Step 8. Then, gently round the sides and end of the blade. Sand the blade lightly, and you're done! I don't usually put finish on my spreaders, but if you choose to, I suggest using salad bowl finish; it puts a nice shine on the wood without adding any toxic ingredients. Allow the finish to dry for 24 hours before using the spreader.

POKER

Small pokers are perfect for serving hors d'oeuvres, including cheese, meat, olives, and pickles. To make one, follow the instructions for the knife through Step 8. Next, flatten all four sides of the blade to form a square, and then cut off the corners and round it, forming the poker shaft. Taper the end of the shaft, making the point slightly off center to avoid the pith.

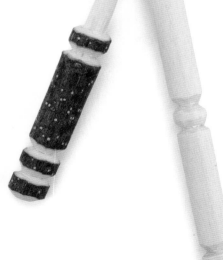

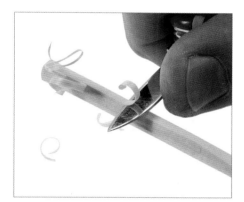

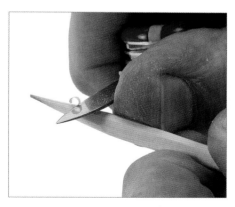

Knife | Victorinox Swiss Army Knife Whittling Book

WHISK

If you stumble across a branch with a bunch of small offshoots, grab it! You've just found a whisk. Cut the main branch about 12" (305mm) long, and trim the shoots to form a nice cluster. Peel the bark off the whisk end and partway up the handle. Round the handle end and cut a decorative groove if you like (page 27, Steps 1–2).

FORK

Forks come in all sizes and can be used to eat, pick up, and roast a number of foods, such as marshmallows and hot dogs. My own versions of forks have three basic components: the handle, the stem, and the fork itself. I've always had just two prongs on my forks, though I'm sure there's no rule against making three or four.

The handle of the fork is exactly the same as that of a knife, so I'm not going to repeat those instructions. See Steps 1–3 on page 27 to refresh your memory.

MATERIALS

- Knife
- Straight-grained stick
- Sandpaper

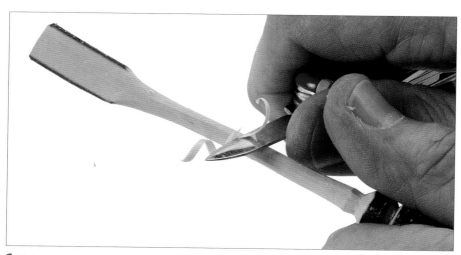

1 Make the handle and flatten the blade as you would for a knife. Then, cutting from both ends toward the center, form the stem of the fork. Leave a little "paddle" at the end. Round the stem.

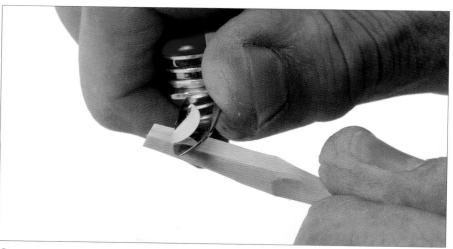

2 Remove the bark from the edges of the "paddle" and taper it to a fairly sharp screwdriver point.

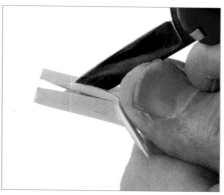

3 Form the prongs by taking out a V-shaped wedge at the tip of the paddle. Insert the knife tip about ½" (13mm) from the end of the paddle section and cut toward the end of the fork. Repeat this motion, always cutting from the point of the V toward the tips of the prongs, to clear out the wedge and form the prongs.

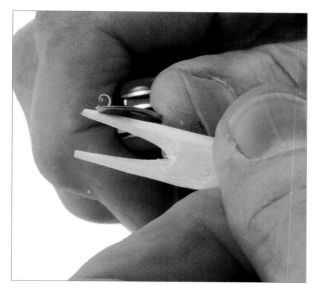

4 Fine tune and sharpen the fork.

The Victorinox factory only uses as much heating oil as a family home. The waste heat from production processes is used to heat the production sites in Ibach-Schwyz, Switzerland, and 120 homes nearby.

Use the knife-handle technique (page 27, Steps 1–3) alone to make an assortment of other projects. Just choose shorter sticks; 3" (76mm) is perfect.

NAME LOGS

Use a ballpoint pen or woodburner to write a name on the log.

NAME PINS

Split a log in half and treat each half as a Name Log. Use epoxy or a good carpenter's glue to stick a pin back to each piece.

PENDANT

Write the name on your log vertically. Bore or drill a hole in the top end and thread the log onto a piece of string.

KEYCHAIN

Make a pendant, but instead of threading it onto string, use a key ring or loose-leaf notepaper ring.

KNITTING NEEDLES

I personally have absolutely no experience with knitting, but I'm told that wooden knitting needles are warmer than metal ones, and quieter, too. Of course, they also work just as well. Whether or not they're actually better for people with arthritis, I honestly don't know, but I will say this: They're easy to make, and it's kind of fun to say, "Look, I made these knitting needles for you!" Who knows, perhaps once you finish this project, you'll be inspired to try your hand at knitting. I've heard that it's also a relaxing pastime, and when you're finished, you have a nice warm scarf or sweater to wear.

MATERIALS

- Knife
- Straight branches or dowels: 2 each 10"-12" (254mm–305mm) long and slightly thicker than you want your needles to be
- Thicker branch
- Sandpaper
- Handsaw or saw on pocketknife
- Wood glue

1 Debark a thin branch, using long, straight strokes. Be sure not to take off too much wood as you slice away the bark.

2 Taper the end of the branch to a point. Not too sharp!

3 Sand the needle smooth. (If you're using a green branch, you'll need to wait until the piece dries a bit before you sand it, in order to get the smoothest result.)

4 Choose a branch the diameter you want for the back end of the needle. Using a handsaw or the saw attachment on your Swiss Army Knife, cut a small slice from the branch and sand both sides smooth. Using wood glue, attach the slice to the end of the needle. Repeat all four steps to make the second needle.

CROCHET HOOK

Although similar in many ways to the other tools we've made in this section, a crochet hook requires a little more finesse with your knife to shape the hook and thumb rest. To help judge the shape you should be making, you might want to use a store-bought crochet hook as a model.

MATERIALS

- Knife
- Straight branch or dowel: 6"–8" (152mm–203mm) long and slightly thicker than you want your hook to be
- Sandpaper
- Pencil

1 Debark the branch. Taper and round the handle end.

2 Flatten a section of the branch about two-thirds of the way from the bottom end of the hook. This is the thumb rest.

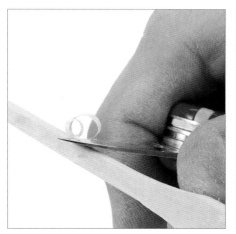

3 Turn the branch 90 degrees and taper both sides of the hook end.

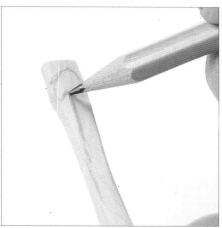

4 Use a pencil to draw the outline of the hook.

The hook on the Swiss Army Knife is also called a "parcel carrier"—put the string of a parcel on the hook instead of your hand to make transportation even easier!

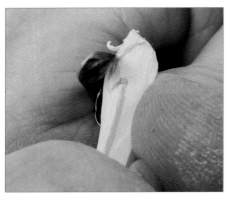 

5 Very carefully carve around the hook outline. Make sure you go slowly as you cut toward the hook; you don't want to slice it off. Using the tip of your blade, notch and shape the hook.

6 Sand the entire crochet hook smooth.

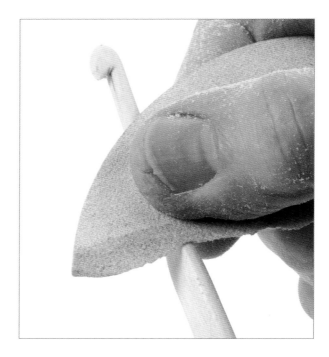

SPOON

It's true what they say—necessity is the mother of invention. This particular project came about when I was set up at a craft show and was getting ready to eat my lunch. As I opened my lunchbox that my wife, Sheri, had so thoughtfully packed for me, I remember being a bit puzzled as to how I was going to eat my yogurt without a spoon. (While good food was on the menu, evidently utensils were not.) Because eating my yogurt with my very, very sharp pocketknife was not the most attractive option, I instead used the knife to carve a 5" or 6" branch into a workable spoon. My yogurt was duly enjoyed, and the spoon is still in one of my little carry-around boxes, waiting for another chance to bail me out of a spoonless situation.

Spoons come in many different styles, shapes, and sizes. The size of the spoon you make will, of course, depend on the size of the piece of wood you start with. You can aim for a smaller mustard or relish spoon or a mammoth pot-stirring spoon for the camp cook. I am demonstrating a teaspoon-sized spoon.

MATERIALS

- Knife
- Straight-grained wood: slightly longer and wider than you want the finished length and bowl of the spoon to be
- Pencil
- Sandpaper: 150- and 220-grit
- Rotary tool (optional)
- Salad bowl finish (optional)

1 Using long, firm strokes, flatten one side of the branch along its entire length. This side will be the top of the spoon.

2 Using a slightly scooping stroke, flatten about two-thirds of the back of the branch, leaving the end thick for making the bowl of the spoon.

3 On the flat side, draw the shape of the spoon.

4 Shape the handle. Cut from the ends toward the center when you do any curved, scooping cuts. If you cut out from the center, you may split the wood where you don't want to.

The JetSetter Swiss Army Knife includes a removable USB flash drive, scissors, ballpoint pen, nail file with screwdriver, letter opener (blade), key ring, and tweezers.

5 Remove the bark from the bowl part of the branch. Shape the bowl of the spoon, cutting off whatever lines you've drawn.

6 Draw the perimeter of the inside of the bowl.

7 With the point of your small blade, very carefully cut inward around the line you've drawn. Be careful to avoid letting your blade slip outward and slice through the outer rim of the bowl.

8 Making lots of repeated V-cuts, hollow out the bowl as much as possible. Naturally, with this type of hollowing out, the inside of the bowl will be quite rough. (Of course, if you happen to have a rotary tool, you can shorten the whole bowl-carving process quite a bit.)

9 Make a bowl-sanding tool by rounding the end of a branch to a shape that will fit nicely into the bowl of the spoon. Wrap a bit of sandpaper around the end of the branch, and sand the inside of the bowl. Sand the entire spoon with fine sandpaper.

From cooking spoons to salt spoons, every size is useful—and no one ever has too many spoons! For a special touch, personalize the handle for your favorite cook.

DIETER'S TASTING SPOONS

These tiny spoons always get a laugh. I carve them out of ½" and ¼" (13mm and 6mm)-diameter dowels and woodburn the words onto the handle. Even the most dedicated dieter can afford a taste this tiny!

CHAPTER THREE

TOYS

Whether you're nine or ninety, or somewhere in between, it's always fun to make a toy. It could be for a special someone else … or even for yourself! I'm a grandpa many times over; sometimes I make toys for my grandchildren, and to be quite honest, sometimes for myself! The giant, 5-foot-tall "Country Pitching Machine" anchored to the roof rack of my minivan is just an overgrown toy, I suppose. I certainly have fun with it, using it very responsibly, of course.

Following are a few suggestions. Both the "Whimmy Diddle" (also called a "Yip Stick," as well as many other names) and the little sailboat require that you drill little holes. Of course, you can use a drill if you have one. However, if you're out in the woods with no drill at hand, look at your Swiss Army Knife—many models are equipped with an awl or reamer that will bore a hole, if you're patient and careful. Also, it's easier to drill or bore a clean hole if the wood is dry, so if your wood is green, let it dry overnight before attempting the holes.

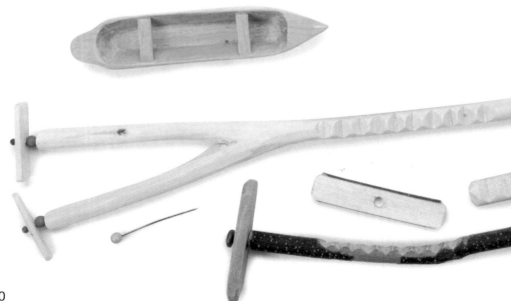

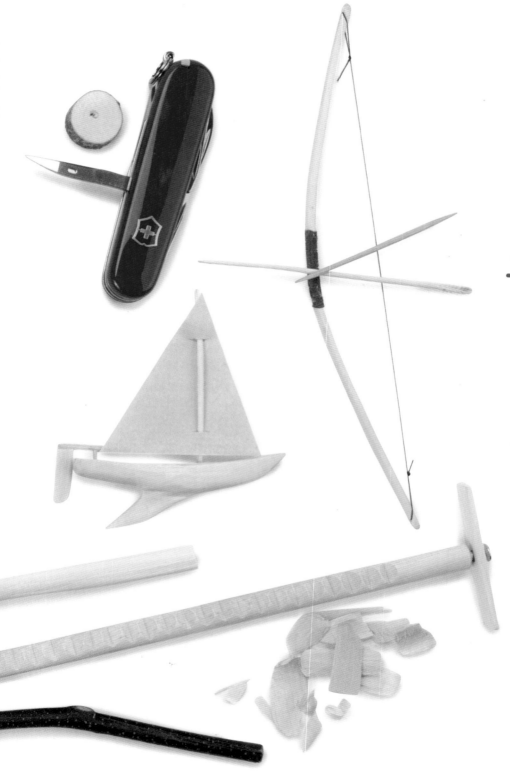

WHIMMY DIDDLE

This super-fun toy has a long history in parts of Appalachia. I often spin "yarns" as to how this little contraption is used by the local mountain folks, but I think I'll save those for my live whittling demonstrations. (My wife constantly chides me for some of the "tall tales" I get people to swallow!) Suffice it to say that when you rub the notched stick with another stick, holding your thumb and forefinger in certain positions against the notched stick, the propeller will spin in one direction, and then, at your command, promptly start spinning the other way. To make a Whimmy Diddle that is more complicated and challenging, use a forked branch and put a propeller at the end of each fork. You'll have to do some adjustment and tweaking of the propeller angles to get them all to work simultaneously.

MATERIALS

- Knife
- Straight stick or dowel: ⅜"–½" (10mm–15mm) dia. x 8"–10" (203mm–254mm) long
- Straight stick: ½"–¾" (13mm–19mm) dia. x 3" (76mm) long
- Small nail, screw, or ball-end pin (one for each fork)
- Craft bead, if you're using a ball-end pin: ⅛" (3mm) dia. (one for each fork; this serves as a washer between the propeller and the stick)

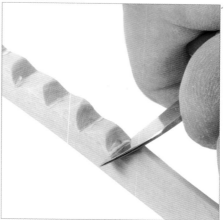

1 Debark the first stick (or if the wood has tight bark, you can leave it on). Make sure one end of the stick is cut flat and smooth; this will be the propeller end. Then hold your knife at about a 45-degree angle and cut a series of V-notches in the stick. Make the notches right next to each other. Notch at least half of the length of the stick.

2 Cut a thin (³⁄₁₆", or 5mm) slice from the center of the shorter stick for the propeller. Round the ends. Drill or bore a small hole in the center of the propeller.

3 Put a pin through the hole and spin the propeller to see if it is balanced; an unbalanced propeller will repeatedly "fall" to the heavy side. Shave or sand the propeller until it is balanced. If you're using a forked stick, make a propeller for each fork.

 In 1998, Play-Doh made a Swiss Army Knife for kids!

4 Thread a craft bead onto the pin next to the propeller, and then press the pin into the flat end of the carved stick. (Drill a hole if necessary.) You may have to bend the pin slightly so the propeller spins freely.

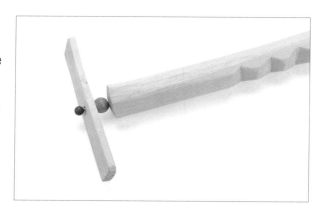

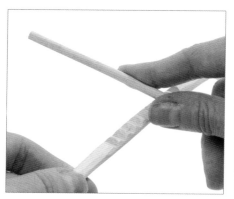

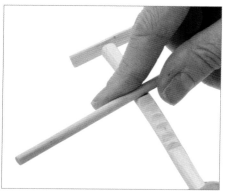

5 Pick up another thin stick and rub it over the notches. Experiment with the way you hold your fingers until the propeller spins. Can you figure out how to make the propeller reverse direction?

SPOILER ALERT! HOW IT WORKS

Hold the rubbing stick in your dominant hand with your forefinger extending over one side of the stick and your thumb on the opposite, lower side of the rubbing stick. There should be about a finger's width separation between your forefinger and thumb. Start rubbing the stick against the notches with your thumb touching the notched stick as you rub. The propeller will spin. Surreptitiously move your hand so your thumb is disengaged and your forefinger is against the notched stick as you rub. The propeller will change directions. Practice the movement until you can do it smoothly and coordinate it with some voice commands (which, truth be told, have absolutely nothing to do with the direction changes...but do make for a good story!).

BOW AND ARROW

I don't remember all of the details, but I do remember the most important part of the event. I was outside a native village just upstream on a little tributary of the Ucayali River, deep in the jungle of eastern Peru. I was eight or nine at the time and was hunting lizards with a young Shipibo boy about my own age. The weapons ... our trusty bows and arrows. There was a lizard lying not too far from my friend's foot. Somehow my aim wasn't too sharp, and I shot the arrow right into his foot ... maybe down by his toes somewhere (at least I hope so). I can't remember exactly what happened after that, but I have a feeling that, the way we kids were, we just pulled out the arrow and went on hunting. It definitely was a different kind of life!

The miniature bow and arrow described here resemble the ones I used to use, but it's on a scale that will serve for the average toy action figure. It won't shoot lizards!

MATERIALS

- Knife
- Bow: Straight stick ¼" (6mm) dia. x 6"–8" (152mm–203mm) long with as few knots as possible and a very small pith (birch is ideal). Don't use a dowel; it is too rigid.
- Arrow: Thin, straight twig 3"–4" (76mm–102mm) long with as few knots as possible
- Carpet thread or heavy-duty sewing thread
- Cyanoacrolate (CA) glue, such as Super Glue®
- Wood glue (optional)

1 Debark the bow stick and thin it evenly all the way around. Slightly flatten two sides until the bow is springy and bendy. Sand it smooth.

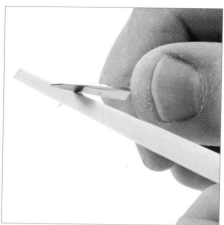

2 On the flat sides of the bow, taper the ends so the top and bottom are thinner than the center. Apply CA glue to the ends to reinforce them, and let the glue dry.

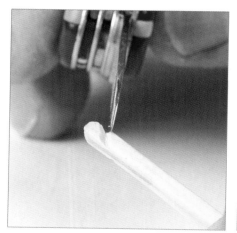

3 Carefully cut a tiny notch in each side of both ends.

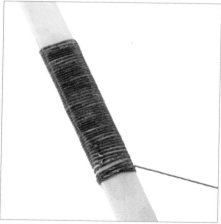

4 (Optional) To form the grip, spread a bit of wood glue on the center of the bow and wrap it with carpet thread.

A Swiss Army Knife is in the collections of the Museum of Modern Art (MOMA) in New York City.

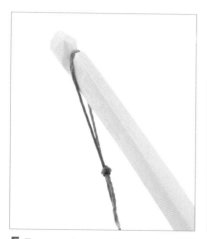

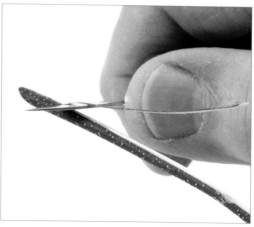

5 To string the bow, tie carpet thread around the notches in one end, bend the bow gently, and knot the thread around the other end.

6 Debark the arrow and thin it all the way around. Sand it smooth.

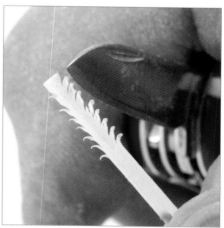

7 Sharpen one end of the arrow to a point. You could carve a notch around the point so it looks more like an arrowhead, or even carve a tiny arrowhead and attach it—but I'm just going to sharpen mine.

8 I use the tip of my knife to fletch the arrow with tiny curls (see page 84 for curl instructions). You could also glue tiny paper vanes to the end. Reinforce the curls or vanes with CA glue.

SAILBOAT

There are a gazillion different styles of sailboats. This one will be yours. Experiment with the proportions of the hull, keel, rudder, mast, and sails to make a boat that you're happy with. Chances are, if you look hard enough, you'll find a "real" boat to match!

The sailboat is definitely one of the more challenging projects in this book. I suggest that you try a few of the others, especially the spoon, before you do this one.

I carved my boat from a small forked branch and a few twigs, but you could also cut the pieces from a block of wood and some very thin dowels, whittle them into shape, and build your boat.

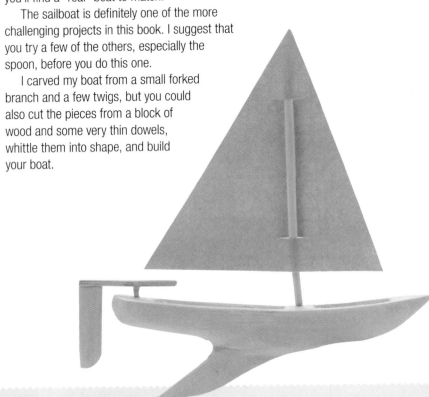

MATERIALS

- Knife
- Forked branch for boat: ⅝"–¾" (16mm–19mm) dia. x 3"–4" (76mm–102mm) long
- Thin stick for tiller: ⅛" (3mm) dia. x 1" (25mm) long
- Thin stick for mast: ⅛" (3mm) dia. x 2½" (64mm) long
- Thicker branch for rudder: ½" (13mm) dia. x 2" (51mm) long
- Pencil
- Rotary tool (optional)
- Drill or knife reamer
- Wood glue
- Paper, cloth, or leaf for sail

1 Flatten the top of the boat branch. Then, remove the bark from the entire branch.

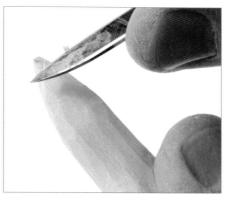

2 Hold the branch by the keel (the small fork), with the fork pointed toward you. The keel points toward the back of the boat. Draw the pointed bow and rounded stern onto the flat side of the branch.

3 Follow your pencil lines and shape the outside of the boat. Round the sides and bottom, but leave the top flat.

"Swiss Army Knife" has become synonymous with something that has it all. An example from the Internet: "Content Repurposing is the Swiss Army Knife of Blogging."

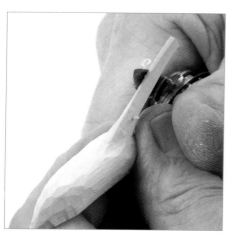

4 Taper the keel from both sides, much the way you tapered the knife blade (see page 29). Round the boat bottom into the top of the keel, being careful not to cut through the keel.

5 Decide how long the keel should be and cut it off at that point. Round the end of the keel. The curve should be on the front (bow) edge of the keel.

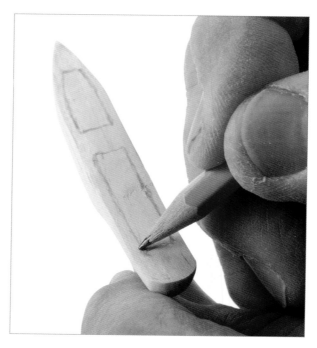

6 Sand the boat. Then, sketch the inside of the hull. I like to make two compartments. I leave extra space at the stern so I have room to install the tiller.

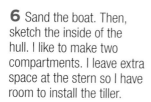

7 Cut around the hull lines with the tip of your knife. Cut a series of criss-crossed lines across the center of each hull space, and then use long, shallow cuts to cut out the chips and hollow the hull. This is similar to hollowing a spoon bowl, but you want the sides and bottom to be straight, not curved. You can speed up the process by using a rotary tool or a small gouge. Then, use a small branch and sandpaper to sand the hollowed hull.

8 To make the rudder, cut the short, thick stick in half, being sure to cut to the side of the pith (just off center). Cut a thin (scant ¹⁄₁₆", or 2mm) slice from the piece with no pith. Debark the sides. Round one short end of the rudder. Carefully shave and sand the flat sides of the rudder so it tapers down to about ¹⁄₃₂" (1mm) thick at the curved end. Cut the rudder off at the desired length; mine is about ¾" (19mm) long.

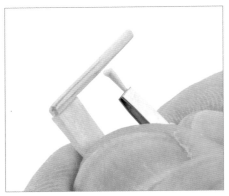

9 Strip the bark off a 1" (25mm)-long twig and round it down to make the tiller (rudder handle). Taper the end of another thin twig down to a splinter that will fit in the tiller hole at the stern of the boat. Cut the splinter off—don't lose it!

10 Glue the rudder to one end of the tiller (I use wood glue). Hold the tiller to the boat, mark the location for the splinter, and glue the splinter to the tiller. (I hold the splinter with my knife's tweezers.) Let the glue dry.

11 Use the awl on the knife to drill small holes in the hull for the mast and tiller. Strip the bark off the mast stick and shave it down until it fits into its hole. Gently put the tiller in place. Cut a piece of paper or cloth—or a leaf—to use as a sail. Bon voyage!

When it comes to carving, a canoe is very similar to a sailboat. Just sketch the shape, round the bottom, and hollow the center. And leave off the keel, of course!

ROWBOAT

A rowboat has a flat bottom and a straight stern, so it's easiest to make one from a piece of milled lumber. Use your knife to split the scrap and saw it to size; my boat is about 3¾" (95mm) long. Draw the pointed bow, and then shape the rowboat just like you did the sailboat. I added a few benches cut from the centers of branches (see Step 8 of the Sailboat) and used the technique for the Fork to make paddles (see page 36).

CHAPTER FOUR

BRANCH ANIMALS

There are all kinds of animals that can be whittled from a forked branch and can be used to top canes or walking sticks, bottle stoppers, or even ballpoint pens. I'll suggest several: horse, donkey, dog, duck, and goat. Other animals call for a straight branch (no fork needed): owl, alligator.

For most of the animals, the forks are inverted, with one of the stems of the Y being left long for the neck (quite extended, to be sure), another cut short for the ears, and the third becoming the nose or muzzle. If you want to make stick bodies for these animals, it's fairly easy to combine smaller twigs or branches for the various parts: the main body, four legs, and a tail.

The Ideal Wood Fork

Because of a wood fork's shape, the grain of the wood runs in three directions from the center of the Y. This feature creates structural strength and results in a final project that is relatively strong, yet flexible, and not easily broken in spite of its delicate appearance. Because of its natural formation, there are some things you can do with a forked branch that you could never do with even the most perfect block of wood because the grain in that block runs in only one direction.

For most branch figures, I think you'll find it a lot easier to work with a wood fork that is free of knots inside the areas marked by the dotted lines. In time, you'll discover that knots and extra branches in certain locations inside these lines don't significantly affect the carving. They may just make the project more challenging, but not impossible.

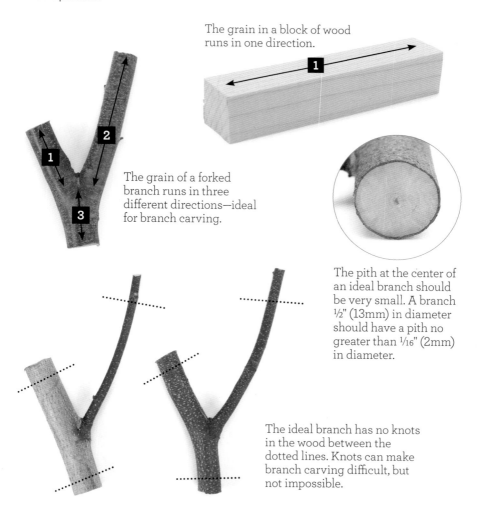

The grain in a block of wood runs in one direction.

The grain of a forked branch runs in three different directions—ideal for branch carving.

The pith at the center of an ideal branch should be very small. A branch ½" (13mm) in diameter should have a pith no greater than 1/16" (2mm) in diameter.

The ideal branch has no knots in the wood between the dotted lines. Knots can make branch carving difficult, but not impossible.

OWL

I started carving owls in 2009 when D. K. Klug of Mobile, Alabama, shared one of his wood-block owls with me. After I figured out how to make a reasonably similar owl out of a round branch, I started playing around with the design. Several years later, and quite a few owls later, I think my technique has improved and my latest owls are quite a bit better than my early efforts. I especially like making the owls and the stumps they're perching on out of the same branch. Folks especially appreciate the mama owl with her owlet sitting on a branch next to her. (Just carve a small owl, flatten a little notch next to "Mom," and glue it in place.)

MATERIALS

- Knife
- Straight branch: This particular branch is 1" (25mm) dia. x 2" (51mm) long. The ideal branch for a simple owl is half as thick as

it is long. Naturally, a branch with a smaller diameter will make a smaller owl.
- Woodburner or pen (optional)

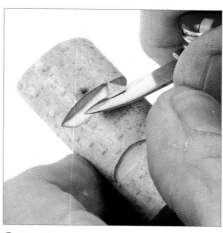

1 Slightly less than a third of the way from one end of the branch, cut three V-notches: one in the center and one on each side. Repeat the notches on the other end. As you push in with the knife, slide it slightly as well; sliding the knife makes it cut more easily.

2 Cut off the two triangle-shaped corners between the notches at the top end to make a smooth groove that goes three-quarters of the way around the top of the owl.

3 In the center front, taper the notch a little bit from the top.

4 Skip a small sliver of bark above the notch you just cut, then taper up toward the top of the head. The bark sliver left in place will be the beak.

In 1997, a Victorinox Swiss Army Knife was used to repair a piano during a concert.

5 That taper you just made? Keep going, but now angle the cut toward the back a little more. Taper the front of the owl up to the midpoint of the head.

6 Turn the owl around and taper the back of the head. Start about even with the front notch. Cut almost straight up, and then go back and taper to the center. The peak at the top of the head forms the horns.

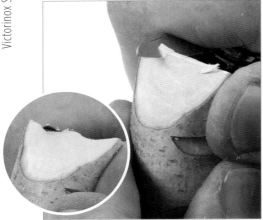

7 At the top of the owl, cut from one corner at a slant. You're aiming toward the center, but only go about a quarter of the way across the head. Repeat on the other side. Then, carve from the center to the edges to form the curve at the top of the head.

8 On each side of the head, maybe ⅛" (3mm) below each horn, cut a sideways V-notch. These notches separate the horns and define the side of the head.

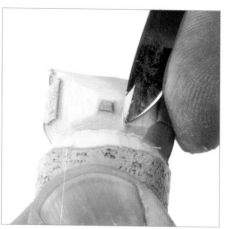

9 Deepen the original notches on the sides of the head. This will help shape the head.

10 Starting with your knife just off center from the beak, taper to the side. Don't cut too far back. Carve from the side toward the beak to remove the chip and shape the side of the head. Repeat for the other side. Leave a bit of bark in the center for the beak.

11 On the back of the owl, about ¼" (6mm) down from the neck notch, make a small horizontal notch to mark the bottom of the tail. Carve vertical notches on each side so the tail meets the front notch on both sides. Use the tip of your knife to carve three V-notches across the tail to represent feathers.

12 The Vs of bark at the bottom front can serve as feet. Or, you can cut off the tips of the Vs and mark three claws on each side with a woodburner and writing tip or a ballpoint pen (don't use a sharpie; it will bleed). Mark the eyes with either the woodburner or pen, as well.

ALLIGATOR

When I was a kid in Peru, my young friends and I used to swim just off the banks of the Ucayali River, one of the main tributaries of the Amazon. Every now and then we'd notice that we weren't exactly alone when we spied a rough nose and two protruding eyes slowly gliding by not too far away. We'd jump back onto the riverbank in a big-time hurry. But then, as soon as our swimming-hole visitor disappeared from view, we'd jump back in. Not too smart for sure! Happily, we're all still around! (As far as I know!)

Just recently, at someone's suggestion and with a little guidance (I honestly don't remember who it was), I carved a few alligators. I'm sure you can improve on the designs, but at least start here.

MATERIALS

- Knife
- Thick, straight branch: ⅝"–¾" (16mm–19mm) dia. x 5½"–6" (140mm–152mm) long

- Woodburner or ballpoint pen. I don't use a felt-tip pen because it tends to spread.

1 Flatten the bottom of the stick.

2 Choose an end for the tail. About two-fifths of the way from your chosen end, taper the flat side toward the end until the tapered portion is past the pith (carve more than halfway through the stick).

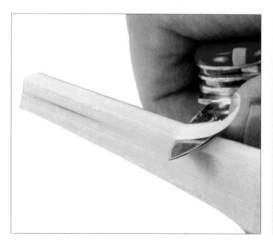

3 Narrow the tail from both sides until it comes to a point at the end. Do not carve the top of the tail (preserve the bark). Taper the underside of the tip of the tail so it's off the ground.

Did you know the Victorinox Swiss Army Knife has orbited the Earth with NASA and has been put to the test at the top of Mount Everest, during North Pole expeditions, and in the deepest rainforest of the Amazon?

4 For the back legs, carve a vertical V-notch on each side of the stick, just in front of the tail. Leave a strip of bark between the tail and the leg notch. Leave another section of bark to represent the leg, and then carve a second vertical V-notch. Make this notch slightly wider (more shallow) on the front side than on the back (tail) side.

5 About one-third of the way from the front of the stick, repeat the notches to form the front legs. The inner notch should be slightly wider toward the back to mirror the back legs.

6 Leave a thin strip of bark in front of the leg, and then narrow the snout of the gator on both sides. Don't come to a point at the tip; the snout is rounded. Then, taper the underside of the snout to lift it off the ground.

Victorinox made Swiss Army Knives specifically for the Boy Scouts of America, complete with the Boy Scouts logo on the handle.

7 Taper the top front of the snout slightly, rounding the tip.

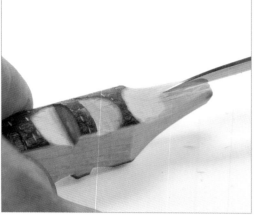

8 Using the tip of the knife, carve a thin, curved line on each side of the snout to represent the mouth. Make the line closer to the bottom of the head; the top jaw is larger than the bottom one. If you're very careful and patient, you could even carve tiny zigzags to look like teeth.

9 Using a ballpoint pen or a woodburner, dot eyes on the top of the gator's head and dot nose holes on the front of the snout. You can darken the mouth lines, too.

ALLIGATOR VS. CROCODILE

According to the San Diego Zoo, alligators live in freshwater swamps, while crocodiles can live in salt water, too. The gator's jaw is rounded, like the letter U; crocs have more pointed, V-shaped snouts. And, finally, only a gator's upper teeth are visible when its mouth is closed. If you can see the bottom teeth, it's a croc.

HORSE PEN

This horse is only one of the animal heads that can be whittled from a forked branch, but it may be my favorite. What we'll be doing here is just carving the head and a rather extended neck. Then, we drill into the neck and insert a ballpoint pen refill.

MATERIALS

- Knife
- Thick forked branch: ⅝"–¾" (16mm–19mm) dia. x 6" (152mm) long. Both forks should be about the same thickness.
- Pencil
- Pen, paint, or woodburner
- Ballpoint pen refill or a cheap pen (one you can easily take apart)
- Hand saw or knife saw
- Drill and assorted sizes of bits

1 Turn the fork upside down. The long piece will be the horse's neck. Draw the ears and rounded muzzle.

2 Use your knife to round the muzzle. Then, take a tiny nick out of the bark on each side of the nose for the nostrils.

3 With the tip of your knife, make a thin V-notch across the front of the muzzle and on each side to form the mouth. A horse's mouth isn't vertically centered, so make the cut in the bottom third of the head. You could also draw, paint, or woodburn the mouth.

4 Cutting from both the front and back of the head, shape the side profiles of the horse's ears.

5 Draw the front view of the ears and cut them. Start near the head and carve toward the tips of the ears, using a process similar to carving the prongs of a fork (see page 37).

6 Mark the eye locations, and then very carefully cut away a small circle of bark for each eye. Use a pen, paint, or a woodburner to draw the eyes and nostrils.

7 Saw the bottom of the horse stick so it's flat. Match a drill bit to the size of your pen's ink refill tube. Carefully drill a hole up the center of the stick. If your stick is green, let it dry for a day or two; it's easiest to drill dry wood.

8 Use a tiny bit to drill a hole through the side of the stick, connecting with the hole in the middle. (The pen won't work without this air hole.) Use the first drill bit to estimate the length of the pen hole and cut the refill tube to fit. Push the tube into the hole, and then carefully taper the wood around the bottom to meet the pen insert.

GOAT

My first goat was a rooster that went wrong. Completely debark the branch. Carve curving horns and a narrow muzzle. Shape the underside of the mouth to add a small beard. Cut almond-shaped ears from another scrap and glue them on.

BACK SCRATCHER

Choose a fork with one really long branch. Use the "neck" as a handle, and scratch your own back with the animal's muzzle or beak!

DOG

Choose a Y-shaped branch. Use one small fork for the ears and the other for the muzzle. Strip the bark farther back on the muzzle, and taper the sides a bit to shape the nose.

DONKEY

A donkey is very similar to a horse, but it has much longer ears. When you cut the fork, leave the main branch longer so you can carve tall ears.

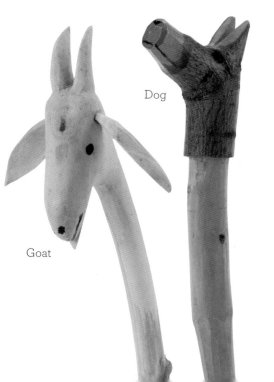

Dog

Goat

Back scratcher

Donkey

Horse Pen | Victorinox Swiss Army Knife Whittling Book

BIRD

A number of years ago, I took one of my neighbor's kids to an Orioles baseball game at the beautiful Camden Yards stadium in Baltimore. As usual I "just happened to have" a few little twigs along for the ride. Sometime during our stay out in the left field corner of the stands, I started to whittle a miniature Baltimore oriole, first using the big oriole on the scoreboard as a pattern and then borrowing my little neighbor's Orioles baseball cap. The little oriole came out pretty well! I think the fans sitting directly behind us got as big a charge out of the oriole carving as they did out of the baseball game.

There are zillions of species of songbirds, and I can't really tell you which one we're doing here. Anyway, let's call this a "generic songbird." For those of you who are into all of the distinctions and subtle nuances of the countless variety of birds, experiment and make the necessary adaptations, both in the carving itself as well as in the painting and finishing.

MATERIALS

- Knife
- Forked branch: Mine is
  ⅝"–¾" (16mm–19mm) dia. x
  4"–5" (102mm–127mm) long
- Pencil
- Sandpaper
- Clear finish, such as polyurethane

1 Remove the bark from the entire branch.

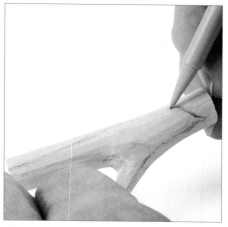

2 Sketch the bird onto the branch. Position the head so the beak runs *with* the grain.

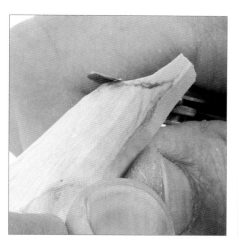

3 Start tapering the head all the way around the branch. Use your lines as a guide. The center of the beak should be close to the center of the branch. There are many different kinds of birds; play with the head and beak proportions to suit yourself.

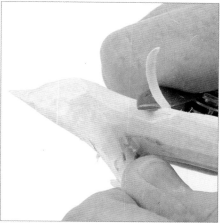

4 Round the chest down to the legs, and taper the front of the legs. Start shaping the body behind the head.

In 2005, a train conductor used a Swiss Army Knife to fix a brake part and restart a stopped train.

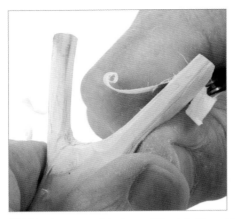
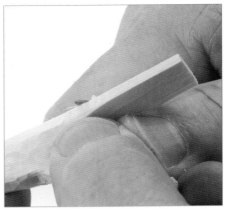

5 Thin the top and bottom of the tail. Round the area where the tail meets the body slightly.

6 Taper the back of the legs. Thin the front of the legs. Thin the sides of the legs slightly and round the tops of the legs into the body.

TINY BIRD

After you've carved a few birds, challenge yourself to see how small you can make one. My grackle is perched on a penny!

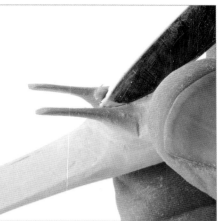

7 Taper the sides of the tail slightly, and round the sides into the body. Decide how long you want the tail to be. Cut the tail to length and round the ends slightly. Then, sand the entire bird.

8 Decide how long you want the legs to be and cut off the excess. Use the technique you used to carve the fork (on page 37) to carve the U-shaped space between the legs.

REFERENCE PHOTOS

Backyard birds come in all different shapes and sizes. If you're trying to carve a specific species, just find a few photos—snap them yourself, check the library, or look online. Sketch the bird's profile onto your branch and start carving! Your version won't be exact, but a little paint can help a robin look more like a robin than, say, a pigeon or a dove.

Starling

Robin

Canary

CHAPTER FIVE

CURL CREATIONS

All of the projects in this chapter call for cutting strokes that result in some kind of "curl"—sometimes very small, other times a little larger, and still others quite long. There are several tricks to carving the best curls, whatever their length. First, of course, your knife blade needs to be properly sharpened and honed. Next, you'll want to adjust the shape of the bevel (the cutting edge) of the blade. You need to know the best time to make the cuts in the wood, and, finally, you just need to practice.

The instructions for these projects can be somewhat convoluted. But, we all know a picture is worth a thousand words and, happily, there are a lot of great pictures!

The Ideal Knife Blade Bevel

The bevel is the tapered edge of the sharpened blade. Many blades have a wedge-shaped bevel that doesn't really cut well and won't make curls. Fixed-blade carving knives often have a very thin, flat bevel that digs in and won't help the wood roll into a curl. I've found that the ideal bevel for both general carving and for making curls has a slight "shoulder," so it curves slightly going down to the sharp edge (see diagram below). It has just enough curve to naturally roll the wood shaving over into a good curl. When you sharpen your knife, slightly round off the corners and bring the bevel up higher on the blade so it tapers more gradually. As you work with your knife and do that normal sharpening and honing, you will come up with the ideal edge.

Blade Cross-Sections

View from the front of the blade's bottom edge (bevel) looking down the blade toward the handle.

Factory-Shaped Bevel

Bevel on Most Fixed-Blade Carving Knives

Curl-Shaped Bevel

The factory-shaped bevel as viewed from the point of the blade toward the handle.

Wet vs. Dry Wood

The amount of curl you get when you carve depends on how wet the branch is. For flowers, trees, and rooster tails, you'll want to use drier wood for more curl. It is nearly impossible to get a good natural curl if the wood is damp or wet, no matter how sharp your blade is or how thin you make the individual slices. However, slight curls are perfect for roadrunner tails. Practice on scrap branches to see the difference.

From right to left, the branches from wettest to driest. The wettest branch doesn't curl. The branch on the far left is the driest, so it curls the most.

Carving Curls

Carving curls isn't hard, once you get the knack. Plan to practice on several small branches before you try a project. You can cut curls with either the small or large blade—use the one you're most comfortable with. Here are a few tips for success:

- Rest the tip of the blade against the twig at a very shallow angle. You don't want to dig into the wood so much as let the edge of the blade lightly catch as you move it.
- Hold the knife firmly and slide the blade forward and slightly down in a short slicing motion. Only cut down ¹⁄₁₆" to ⅛" (2mm to 3mm). Do not cut straight down; you aren't peeling a carrot!
- Draw the knife back without cutting—you are not sawing. Don't lift the blade, either, because lifting the blade starts a new cut.
- Make another tiny, controlled, forward slice as you push down slightly on the knife. The knife tip should move both right-left and down in this movement.
- Pull the blade back and repeat the forward cut. It might take seven or eight tiny cuts to make one curl.

Note: All instructions are for right-handed carvers. Lefties just need to reverse the instructions.

Curl Tricks

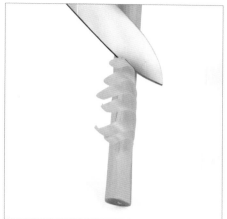

To make a straight curl, like for a rooster tail, hold the knife straight across the branch and cut down. The wood will curl down in line with the stick.

To make curls that bend to the right, tip the knife blade down as you cut.

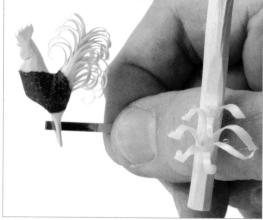

For curls that bend to the left, tip the knife blade up.

Combine cutting styles to create a curl explosion!

 In Portland, Oregon, a man used the tweezers on his Victorinox Swiss Army Knife to escape a fiery elevator.

FLOWER

Some of the quickest projects I carve are little flowers, complete with petals, stem, and leaves. I've given away many thousands of tiny, unpainted flowers over the years. I whittle them from scraps left over from making the tails on my roosters, pheasants, and roadrunners. Other times I'll start with a plain twig, or even a toothpick. Each flower takes little more than a minute to make, but the person to whom I give it is usually pleased way beyond what my little bit of work deserves.

Because moisture really affects the flower petals, you need to be careful if you paint a flower. Oil paints are fine to use, but acrylic paint straight from the bottle will cause the petals to uncurl! If you want to use acrylics, just "paint" the flower with cyanoacrylate (CA) glue, such as Super Glue®, first. Let the glue dry and then add the color.

MATERIALS

- Knife
- Straight-grained, partially dry twig: 1/16"–1/4" (2mm–6mm) dia.
- Oil paints or acrylic paints and cyanoacrylate (CA) glue, such as Super Glue®
- Clear finish, such as polyurethane

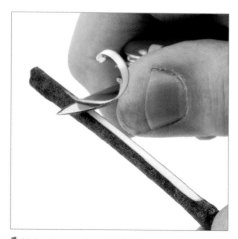

1 Using long, straight strokes, remove the bark from the branch.

2 Starting a short distance from one end of the twig and using the tip of your small blade, carve down to form the first petal.

3 Turn the twig a tiny bit and carve another petal next to the first. Carve petals around the branch, always cutting down to the same depth.

4 Carve another layer or two of petals. Try to position the petals in the subsequent layers between the petals of the previously carved layer.

5 Twist out the little central core that's left in the middle of the flower.

6 Taper down the stem, bringing it into better proportion in relation to the size of the flower. (Of course you can always leave the stem thick. Then you have a little palm tree!)

7 Carve down a couple more little curls to serve as the leaves.

8 "Pick" the flower at the bottom of the stem. The petals are fairly sturdy, so feel free to position them where you want. If you're going to paint the flower, coat it with cyanoacrolate (CA) glue. Otherwise, just poke a hole in a piece of bark or mulch and "plant" the flower in its base.

TIP

Some carvers prefer to leave the bark on the branch in order to give the outside ring of petals a different look. If you decide to do this, make sure the wood you're using has tight bark that won't just fall off after the flower dries out.

TREE

The little trees I make are somewhat similar to the well-known carved trees that are found in Germany, in that the branches and trunk come from a single piece. The German trees that I've seen, however, have rings of branches that come into the trunk at the same level and are quite a bit larger than the little trees illustrated here. You'll notice that the branches on these miniature trees come down in a spiral.

While the tree itself will only be about 2" (51mm) tall, I like to use a longer stick so I have something to hold while I carve. Use a straight stick that has no knots anywhere along the tree portion (knots on the "handle" portion are fine).

MATERIALS

- Knife
- Straight-grained stick: ¼" (6mm) dia. x 6" (152mm) long
- Cyanoacrylate (CA) glue, such as Super Glue®
- Polyurethane or other clear finish (optional)

1 With long, straight strokes, remove all of the bark. Then, taper the point of the branch—sort of like sharpening a pencil the old-fashioned way.

2 With the thumb of the hand that's holding the knife braced against the fingers of the hand that's holding the branch, make very small, controlled shaving cuts toward the point of the stick to form branches.

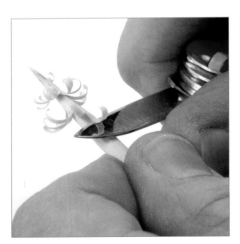

3 Turn the stick slightly as you make each new branch. Each one will be the slightest bit longer than the preceding one as the branches spiral down the trunk.

4 As you carve down the trunk, keep your blade-holding thumb braced against your wood-holding hand. This helps you control the cuts. If you try to freehand a cut, there's a good chance you'll lose control and slice off several branches.

In Vis, Croatia, a doctor lost his Victorinox Swiss Army watch in the ocean. Two months later, a diver found it, still running. The watch had an engraving on the back, so the diver returned it to its owner.

5 Dot the bases of the branches with a bit of cyanoacrolate (CA) glue. The glue soaks in and reinforces the branches, preventing breaks.

6 Chop down the tree. I make small V-cuts all the way around the stick, which makes it easy to cut through.

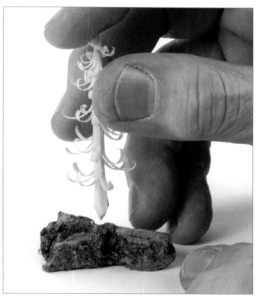

7 I like to "plant" my trees in bark bases. Use the tip of the blade or your knife's awl to make a hole in the bark.

8 Glue the tree in place, checking it from all angles to make sure it's standing straight.

ROOSTER

The majority of my whittled critters are roosters of all shapes and sizes, so I've frequently been asked, "Why so many roosters?" There are several simple and practical reasons that the mascots of my branch carving are indeed roosters. First, they're the first thing (outside a slingshot!) that I remember seeing carved from a Y-shaped branch. Second, the rooster is perhaps the only bird that walks around with its tail *up*. (Turkeys and peacocks can strut, but their normal tail position is *down*.) Third, roosters are popular worldwide, and it seems that folks everywhere appreciate them. Finally, I like to teach roosters because you will learn most of the basic cuts and techniques that will be used in producing other projects. Once you have the rooster-carving technique down, it's not that hard to switch over to herons, roadrunners, and a whole pile of other critters and projects. Hence, roosters!

MATERIALS

- Knife
- Forked branch: The head-foot section is 2½" (64mm) long and about ⅝" (16mm) in diameter. The tail branch is about 4" (102mm) long and ¼" (6mm) in diameter.
- Sandpaper
- Oil or acrylic paint: red, yellow, black
- Paintbrush

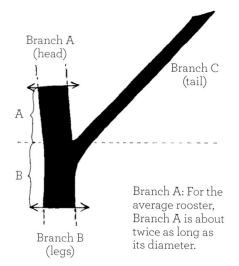

Branch A
(head)

Branch C
(tail)

1 You can make any size rooster by looking for branches based on their proportions rather than their measurements.

A

B

Branch B
(legs)

Branch A: For the average rooster, Branch A is about twice as long as its diameter.

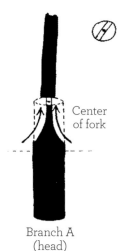

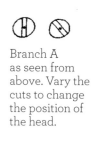

Branch A as seen from above. Vary the cuts to change the position of the head.

Center of fork

Branch A
(head)

2 Taper the sides of Branch A to form the rooster's head and neck. Stop before you get to the pith on each side.

 In Indonesia, a man used his Swiss Army Knife to save his own life when he choked on a fishbone. He used the integrated pliers to pull the bone out of his own throat!

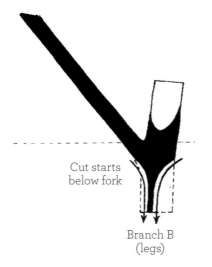

Cut starts
below fork

Branch B
(legs)

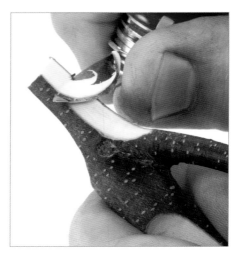

3 Turn the branch 90 degrees. Scoop and flatten the front and back of Branch B to form the rooster's legs. Carve past the pith on the front so you take more wood from the front than the back; this will give your rooster a puffed chest.

4 Use long, smooth strokes to remove the bark from all of the branches, leaving only the rooster's "vest" of natural bark. For an all-white rooster, you can remove all of the bark.

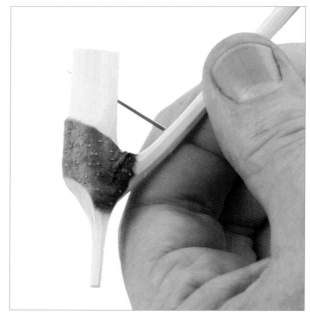

5 Starting at the center of Branch B, cut two arches down and away from the body of the rooster to shape the legs. This is just like making the prongs of a fork; see page 37 for detailed instructions. Round the legs as you taper them.

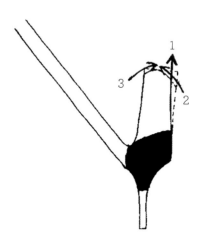

6 Shape the rooster's head by making three separate cuts. Cut 1: Remove a small amount of wood from the front of Branch A. Cut 2: Make a slightly curved cut from the front to the top center. Cut 3: Make a curved cut from the back of the head toward the top center. Make the angle of cut 2 a bit steeper than the angle of cut 3.

 In 1997, a fisherman tangled in a shrimp net used his Swiss Army Knife to cut the rope and save himself from drowning.

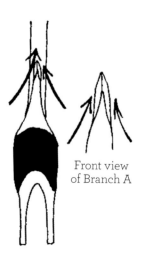

Front view
of Branch A

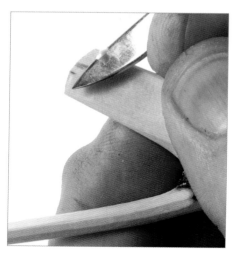

7 Taper the sides and sharpen the top of Branch A to form the rooster's comb.

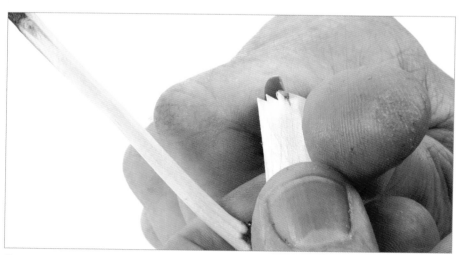

8 Shape the comb by cutting tiny V-notches across the top. Make a cut at a 45-degree angle first, and then free the chip with a cut at a 90-degree angle.

ROOSTER PROJECT NOTE

Especially on steps 9, 10, and 12 of this project, cut only a little at a time, making a cut 1 followed by a cut 2, and repeating these cuts as many times as necessary to get the desired shape. It's much better to make a number of shallow cuts than to dig in too deeply and end up splitting your project.

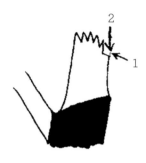

9 Form the front of the comb and the top of the beak by making the two cuts shown in the diagram. For cut 1, wiggle the wood onto the knife instead of pushing the knife into the wood—you'll have more control. Make cut 2 carefully so you don't cut off the beak.

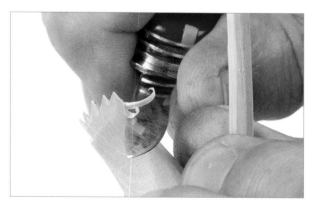

10 Make the two cuts shown in the diagram to form the back of the rooster's neck and comb. Refer to the Rooster Project Note above before making these cuts.

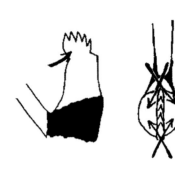

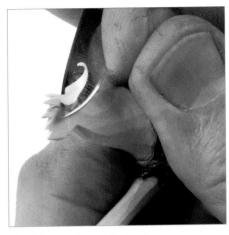

11 Taper from the sides to sharpen both the back of the comb and the beak.

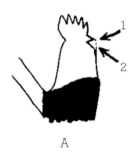

A

B

C

12 Cut a V-notch below the beak (A). Then, cut a V-notch below the wattles (B). Finally, round the wattles and smooth the neck (C).

First-century Romans created the first folding pocketknife, but it fell out of favor when sheathed knives became more popular. The pocketknife regained popularity in the 16th century, especially in the American colonies.

13 Split the wattles by making a thin V-cut with the tip of your knife blade.

14 Now we're ready to do the tail. Before attacking the tail branch of the rooster you're carving, practice on a scrap branch that is the same size as the rooster's tail branch. Secure the end of the branch by tying it to a non-slip surface. Use short, repeated, forward-slicing motions to produce thin curls of wood (see page 84). Make the strips as thin as possible without actually slicing them off. If your rooster is carved from fresh wood, allow it to dry for a bit and use your test branch to ensure it's ready to cut.

15 Now that you've practiced, use the same method on the rooster itself. Remember, use short, repeated, forward-slicing motions. It might take seven or eight slices to cut to the bottom of one feather curl. Make sure you take the cuts all the way down to the base of the tail branch.

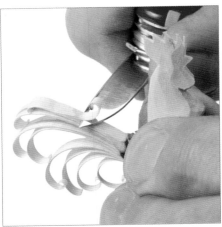

16 When you've made the last feather (the top one), thin it a little, cutting from the bottom up.

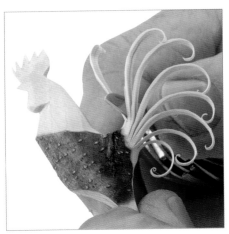

17 With the flat surface of your small blade, spread the feathers apart into the position in which you want them to stay.

18 Paint the rooster with red, yellow, and black acrylic paint. Do the yellow first and then the red so you can cover any mistakes. Dot the eyes with black. It can be helpful to hold the rooster upside down to paint it, so you get crisp edges on your paint lines.

Once you master the basic rooster, branch out and see what else you can do. I have made tall, small, skinny, and even two-headed roosters! Play with the curls, too, by mixing them up and putting them in unexpected places.

PHEASANT

To make a pheasant, turn a rooster branch upside down. When you carve the head, leave off the comb and wattles. Carve the tail while it is still wet; you don't want much curl.

101

HEN

The carving strokes and techniques to make a hen are similar to that of the rooster, but there are some differences.

MAKE A NEST

First, carve a hen without legs. Flatten the bottom slightly. Make a puddle of wood glue and drop some wood shavings, sawdust, or dried grass on top. Put a little glue on the bottom of the hen and nestle her into place.

Unlike the rooster, you'll want to use a branch with forks of equal thickness. You can see the difference between a rooster branch (right) and a hen branch (left) in the above photo. In this project, I used a branch with forks about ½" (13mm) in diameter.

The hen's comb and wattles are different from the rooster's; the comb is shorter, and the wattles are smaller.

Unlike the rooster's curled tail, the hen's tail is carved to a point. To carve the hen's tail, debark from the backs of the legs up the tail fork. Taper the sides of the tail and flatten the back. Work into the branch from three sides until you cut it off. Point and shape the tail.

Pocketknives were essential tools for soldiers throughout American history—even George Washington carried one!

Rooster | Victorinox Swiss Army Knife Whittling Book

CHICK

Make a family of chickens by carving any number of baby chicks. You could carve a whole flock from one well-branched twig. The front and side drawings (at right) should give you an idea of what to do.

Karl Elsener opened his original cutlery workshop in Ibach-Schwyz, Switzerland, in 1884 with the support of his mother, Victoria.

BASES FOR BIRDS AND
OTHER BRANCH ANIMALS

The base or setting you use for the figure you've just carved can make all the difference in the world. The variety is almost endless. Knotholes, gnarled pieces of bark, weathered stumps, chunks of firewood, vines...the list goes on. Each base serves a different purpose or sets the rooster or branch animal off in a different way. Over the years I've been absolutely amazed at some of the settings different people have made for their carvings.

HERON

While I'm calling this particular bird a heron, I suppose it's really a sort of generic, long-legged, tall, slender waterfowl. You can call it an egret, too, or whatever else you decide to make it. The forks used for herons need to be straight-grained, and should be inverted when you carve. The long A and B branches should be without knots.

MATERIALS

- Knife
- Forked branch (see Step 1 for size notes)
- Sandpaper
- Oil or acrylic paint: orange-yellow, black
- Paintbrush

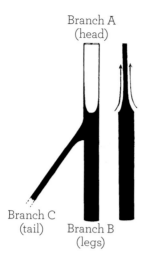

Branch A
(head)

Branch C
(tail)

Branch B
(legs)

1 Cut the branch to size. On my sample carving, the main branch, which forms the head and legs, should be ⅜" (10mm) in diameter and 4¼" (108mm) long. The tail fork should be ¼" (6mm) in diameter and centered on the thick branch; the length isn't critical. Taper the sides of Branch A for the head and neck. Don't begin your cuts too low if you want the heron to have a natural bark "vest." An all-white, "barkless" heron looks good, too.

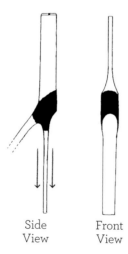

Side
View

Front
View

2 Turn the branch 90 degrees and taper Branch B to form the legs. Take more wood from the front than from the back. Trim the bark from the legs, body, and tail, leaving some to create the heron's natural vest. Take a little wood off the outsides of the legs as you remove the bark.

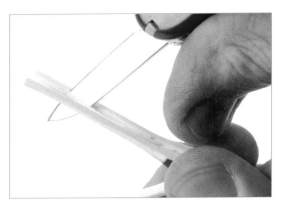

3 Think of the heron legs as a long fork (see page 37). To separate the legs, start at the top of the legs and cut toward the feet. Make these cuts on both the front and the back. Very carefully round the legs. Go slowly. It's very easy to let your blade slice diagonally and cut off a leg.

TIP

To avoid a diagonal cut that will slice off the long legs, brace the knife against the edge of the table. Lay the edge of the heron on its side and slide the wood along the knife. Once you have made the first cut, it's much easier to thin the legs.

4 Shape the heron's neck. Follow the arrows on the diagram indicating the direction of the cuts. If you don't respect the direction of the grain, you'll end up cutting away more wood than you planned.

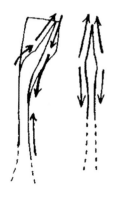
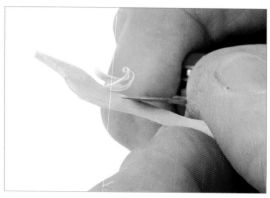

5 Shape the head and beak. Once again, watch the direction of these cuts. If you catch the grain the wrong way, it will be very easy to accidentally cut off the beak or even a good part of the head.

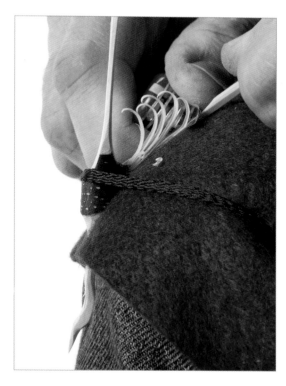

6 Carve the heron's tail. Position the heron at the very end of your knee, even closer to the end of your knee than the rooster. By positioning the heron so the head and neck hang over your knee, you will be relieving some of the pressure that will be put on them as you make the tail slices. Make short slices, similar to the rooster, starting with the shortest feather (the one closest to the back legs).

7 After cutting through the tail branch, you need to thin the last feather a bit. Always cut away from the heron's body toward the tip of the feather. Then, separate and position the feathers as you want them.

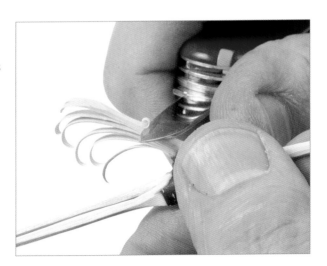

8 Round and smooth the heron's head, beak, neck, and legs. This is best done when the carving is dry and the wood has firmed up more. For this step, you may want to use a tiny piece of fine sandpaper. Or you can scrape these parts lightly with the knife blade, being careful not to lift the grain. Paint the beak, legs, and eyes.

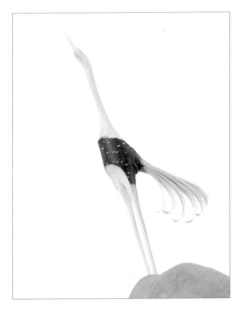

In 1891, Karl Elsener and his coworkers delivered knives for Swiss Army soldiers for the first time.

ROADRUNNER

I rather doubt that any pure-blooded, self-respecting Southwest roadrunner would agree that it looks like the one we're going to make here, but maybe the little guy that runs around in cartoons, chased in every conceivable way by a certain coyote, will see a cousin.

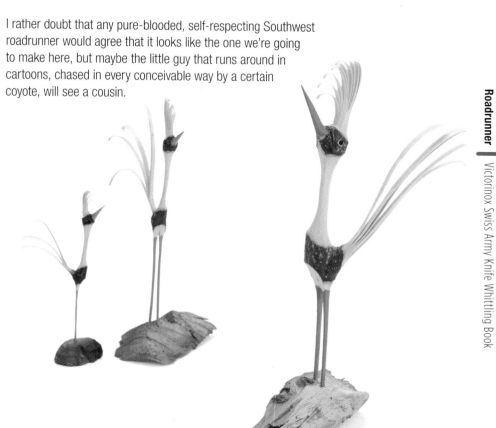

MATERIALS
- Knife
- Double-forked branch
  (see Step 1 for size notes)
- Sandpaper
- Oil or acrylic paint:
  orange, black
- Paintbrush

1 The roadrunner requires a branch with two forks, one above the other. It's especially important that Branches C (tail), B (legs), and A (neck) are long, straight, and without knots or extra branches. Branch E (beak) need not point straight ahead. It can be turned to one side or the other, or even backwards! On my sample branch, the main section is 6½" (165mm) long and about ½" (13mm) in diameter. The tail branch is about 5½" (140mm) long.

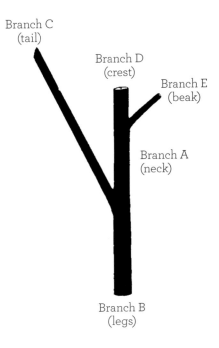

Branch C
(tail)

Branch D
(crest)

Branch E
(beak)

Branch A
(neck)

Branch B
(legs)

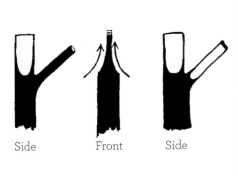

Side   Front   Side

2 Taper both sides of Branch D for the "top knot." Start at the top fork and scoop in and up. Then, taper both sides of Branch E for the beak.

Karl Elsener registered the iconic cross and shield emblem as a trademark in 1909.

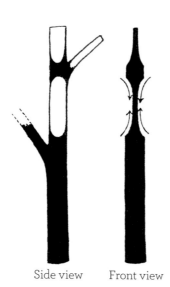

Side view   Front view

3 Taper the sides of Branch A toward the middle to shape the neck. Make sure to follow the directions of the arrows on the diagram. Notice where the cuts start and where the bark is left intact.

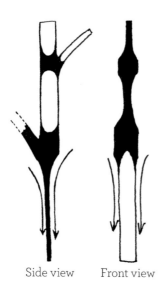

Side view   Front view

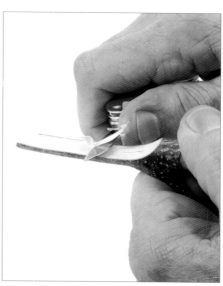

4 Rotate the branch 90 degrees and taper the front and back of Branch B for the legs. Take more wood from the front than the back. Make sure you carve the curve at the top of these cuts so the roadrunner's chest will stand out.

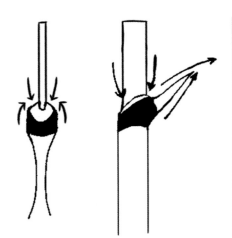

5 Shape the beak and the top of the head. Sharpen the beak. Round the top of the head with tiny V-notches to separate the head from the crest. Trim the bark to complete the top of the roadrunner's mask.

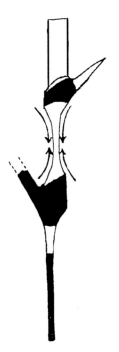

6 Shape the front and back of the roadrunner's neck. Round and smooth the neck and taper the bark neatly into the wood at the base of the neck where it joins the body and at the top of the neck where it joins the head.

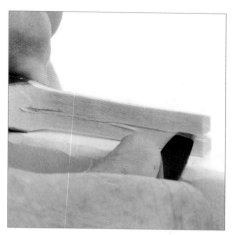

7 Debark the outside of each leg. Then, as with the heron (see page 108), think of the legs as a long fork. Start at the top and cut toward the feet. To make the first cut, brace the knife against the table, insert the knife, and slide the wood along the blade.

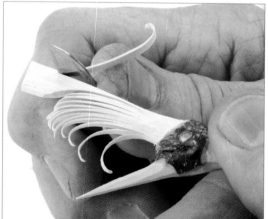

8 Cut out the eye holes in the mask.

9 Debark the tail. Then, carve the top knot. Make downward strokes toward the head, similar to carving the flower. Start in the front to make the curls curve forward, or start from the back to make the curls curve backward. You could also just skip the curls and carve a series of notches like the rooster comb (see page 111). If the limb is really thick, shave some wood off the front or back and cut off the excess.

10 Carve the roadrunner's tail. You only need a few feathers. For this long tail, we don't want a lot of curl, so I make long carving strokes from top to bottom. Shorter strokes will produce curlier feathers.

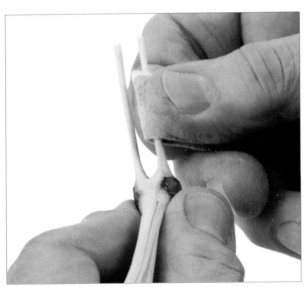

11 Finish the roadrunner. Bend the tail feathers toward the back of the roadrunner's neck, positioning them however you think looks best. Smooth the legs and neck with very fine sandpaper or by lightly scraping the surface with your knife blade. Paint the beak and legs orange-yellow and the eyes black. Spray with clear finish if you like.

 In 1921, Karl Elsener coined the company's name "Victorinox" by combining his mother's name, Victoria, with "inox," an abbreviation of the French word for rust-resistant steel, "inoxydable."

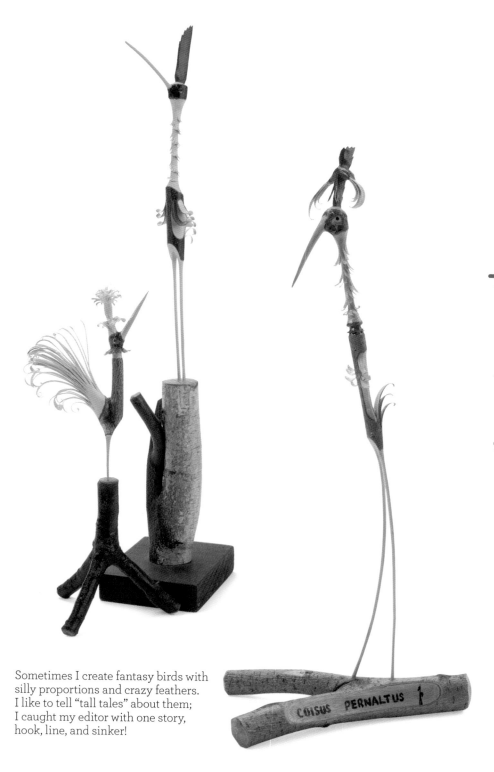

Sometimes I create fantasy birds with
silly proportions and crazy feathers.
I like to tell "tall tales" about them;
I caught my editor with one story,
hook, line, and sinker!

117

SQUIRREL

All kinds of feelings come over me when I think of squirrels. On the positive side, my family and a friend from Portugal had great fun with the super-tame and friendly squirrels that ate right out of our hands in the middle of Washington, D.C. My boarding-school roommate and I kept a pair of flying squirrels in our dorm room in Asheville, North Carolina, until our headmaster made us expel them. The pair had babies, which we would let run around inside our shirts!

But then there's the destructive gray squirrel who, a number of years ago, chewed his way through a wall of my treehouse, panicked, and then tried to chew his way out through the window frames. (My pocketknife came in handy to smooth out all the damage he had done. My window frames are now somewhat rounded!)

I owe the squirrel idea to Shep Rexrode of York, Pennsylvania. As a participant in a whittling contest twenty or so years ago, Shep showed up with a branch rooster yelling at a branch squirrel that was sitting on a fencepost, "Crow, or get off the post!" Years later, Shep's widow gave that same little squirrel to me. Needless to say, I felt very honored and grateful. The following is my own attempt at a fun little critter like the one Shep so creatively whittled.

MATERIALS

- Knife
- Forked branch (see Step 1 for size notes)

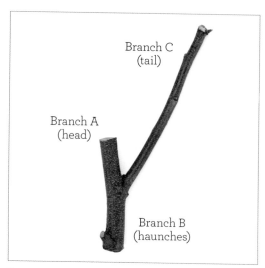

Branch C
(tail)

Branch A
(head)

Branch B
(haunches)

1 A squirrel branch is similar in shape to a rooster branch. However, the bottom of the main branch should be a little longer, to accommodate both the squirrel's body and his post, and the tail branch needs to be a larger diameter to create the fluffy tail (mine is around ⅜", or 10mm, in diameter).

2 Remove most of the bark from Branches A and C. Leave some bark on the front of Branch A for the nose and acorn.

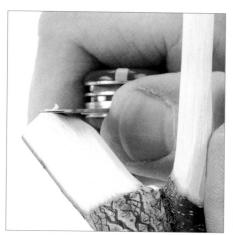

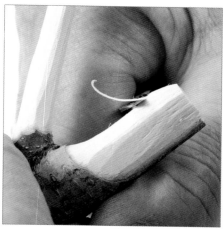

3 On the back of Branch A, carve up at an angle on the top to shape the back of the head and the ears.

4 Make a scooping cut on the back to create a bit of a curve up to the angled cut.

5 On the front, carve up at an angle to create the forehead and to make a point on the end for the ears. The ears should be slightly closer to the back of the branch than to the front (slightly off center toward the back).

6 Make two little V-notches to shape the sides of the ears. Leave the branch end higher in the middle for the rounded head. After you cut the ears to the right length, round the top of the head.

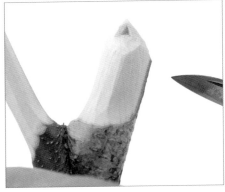

7 Make a long V-notch to taper the outside of the ears and round the face. The tips of the ears stick out past the sides of the face. Then, round the face up to the spot where the ears attach to the head.

8 To carve the insides of the ears, use the tip of the knife to remove a small triangle-shaped chip. The chip should be deepest in the center.

Victorinox sells more than just pocket knives—they also sell household and professional knives, watches, travel gear, apparel, and fragrances!

9 Make a V-shaped cut on both sides of the head to separate it from the arms. Carefully round the sides of the head into the bottom of the V-notch.

10 Extend the V-shaped cuts from the sides onto the front to separate the nose and chin from the arms. Leave the bark on the tip of the nose to give the squirrel a little black nose. Taper the sides of the face in toward the tip of the nose.

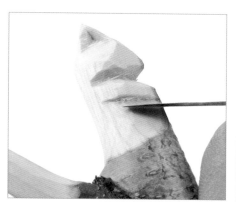

11 Make a cut along the bottom of the arms on both sides, and then taper the body up to the cut to separate the arms from the body. The arms are flatter where they attach to the shoulders and stick out more as they move closer to the front.

12 Leave the bark on the front of the hands for the acorn. Make a deeper cut on the front where the arms stick out more, holding the acorn. Taper the belly up to the cut. Round the acorn without cutting the bark off.

13 Make a V-notch the whole way around the bottom of the haunches (similar to the V-grooves carved around the handle of the knife; see page 27).

14 Make a hard cut straight in around the top and front of outline of the haunches. Leave the bark on the haunches, and carve the body toward the outline to shape the haunches and separate them from the body.

15 Remove the bark from the back of the body, but leave the bark on the joint of the branch. Taper the bottom of the haunches down to where they meet the base.

16 Deepen the two cuts straight in along the front of the haunches as you approach the base. Carefully remove wood from between the cuts, outlining the haunches. This creates a groove that gets deeper as you round the belly toward the base and the feet. The haunches stick out more near the base. Then, round the belly down into the cut along the haunches. As with the rooster, if you're working with a fresh branch, at this point, let the tail branch dry so the little furry things curl. If the branch is too wet, the tail pieces will not curl properly.

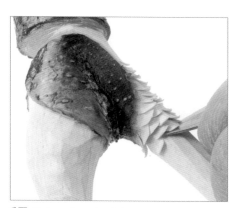

17 Make a bunch of tiny cuts at the base of the tail to represent the short bushy fur at the base. These cuts can have a small amount of curl, but they are more for texture than anything else. Use the thumbpushing technique explained on page 19. Make these cuts up to about one-third the final length of the tail.

18 Finish carving the tail. As you work your way up, gradually increase the length of the cuts and add more curl to the cuts. Use a thumbpushing cut as you essentially carve long branches on an upside-down tree on the squirrel's tail (see page 89).

19 As you carve toward the core of the branch, make the curls progressively smaller. You are basically making a small flower at the tip of the tail. When the branch gets thin enough, twist it off like you did for the flower (see page 88).

20 To petrify the tail in position, wet the curls with cyanoacrolate (CA) glue where they join the base. Smooth the belly and body a little with sandpaper if you like.

21 Mark the positions of the eyes and feet with a pencil to make sure they are symmetrical. I use a woodburner to add the eyes and feet, but you could use a pen.

22 To add a base, first make sure the bottom of the squirrel's stump is flat. Hold a piece of sandpaper flat on the table and carefully sand the bottom flat and smooth. I just glue the bottom of the branch to a larger round slice of a branch to give the squirrel and its stump more stability.

Squirrels can be big or small, light or dark. Have fun making an assortment!

CHAPTER SIX

SIMPLE BUT STUNNING

It's amazing to see the almost infinite variety of things a person can make with wood, and often with relatively little actual "work"! Often the very piece of wood itself suggests a special use or subject. Unique branch shapes, bark and grain patterns, and varying colors within the wood all lend themselves to beautiful works of art, and some to very practical and useful objects.

The more you are around wood and work with it, the easier it will be to spot these special pieces. Sometimes you'll discover a branch with all kinds of personality—a hollow stump, a unique knothole, or even a tiny twig—and you won't know *yet* what to do with it, but you'll pick it up and save it … because *someday* you'll know just what it should be! I've had that experience many times!

Keep your eyes wide open. Observe. Have fun. Create!

TABLE ART

Occasionally, I'll stumble across a chunk of found wood that just screams to be plunked down in the middle of a coffee table and called modern art. In your searches for nifty pieces of wood, you might find something that is just plain cool all by itself. In that case, I recommend cleaning it up and letting it speak for itself!

Find an interesting piece of wood. A good place to look, if you want to find a piece of wood like the one shown in this project, is anywhere large bushes are being removed. The core area of a bush where the branches diverge will look like this piece of yew. Clean up the wood using water and a scrub brush until all of the dirt is removed. Cut the branches until you've shaped the tangle of branches in a way that is pleasing to you. Sand the sawn faces of the branches. Finish as desired.

Once you clean it up, the core of a bush makes an artistic table decoration.

UTENSIL AND JEWELRY TREES

Trees and bushes get pruned or cut down for all kinds of reasons, and the interesting branches you find on the ground can turn into beautiful, original, and useful pieces. Mounted on a base, these branches are perfect for organizing, storing, and displaying cooking utensils in the kitchen and jewelry in the bedroom.

Trim the branches to suit your needs, and then use a screw through the bottom to mount it on a base, such as a log slice or a piece of milled lumber. Apply clear spray finish if you like. Sometimes you might want to add some cup hooks. Other times you won't need to add anything to the branch for it to serve its purpose.

SIMPLY SLICES

Wood slices have so much potential—here are just a few of the things you can do with them. For the most part, all you need to do is saw slices and then sand them. You can use the saw on a Swiss Army Hiker for thinner branches. Make sure the branches you saw your slices from are well seasoned. If you slice a fresh or green branch, the pieces are almost certainly going to split as they dry. A 90-degree cut will produce round slices, and an angled cut will give you oval shapes.

Coasters

The basic idea of a coaster is to provide a flat, stable surface for a glass, cup, or mug that will protect the table surface from heat or liquid damage (or both). These coasters are extremely simple to make and will fulfill their intended purpose, but at the same time, they're a bit out of the ordinary—they're original pieces of useful decoration. Different species of wood will produce a broad variety of cross-grain patterns and colors. These will especially stand out when the sliced pieces of wood are well sanded.

Checkers

One of the most universally known games is checkers. Granted, different parts of the world have different rules. If you're used to American rules and you're playing someone from Europe or South America, watch out for "flying kings"! In all cases, though, the board and checkers are the same. I have made a number of sets, some enormous (one board, cut from the trunk of an elm, is 4', or 1,219mm, wide) and others quite small. The saw blade on the Swiss Army Hiker will do a good job of cutting the checkers. Color one set of pieces with either wood stain or a permanent marker and leave the other set natural. When you make the board with its 64 squares, color alternating spaces.

Necklaces

Twigs and branches exist in all kinds of sizes, colors, bark textures, and grain patterns. By cutting various-sized slices from different species of wood, or even from different-sized wood of the same species, you can make a good variety of natural wood beads. By stringing them together, you can come up with a very attractive and unique necklace.

Tic Tac Toe

I make tic tac toe sets two ways. If you're out in the woods looking for something to do, you can use a Swiss Army Hiker to cut slices of a branch. Mark some of them with an X (the round branch is a natural O), draw a board on a piece of paper or on the ground, and start playing.

If you have a drill available, you can make a travel set. Cut a slice from a thicker branch and use your knife to score lines into the top for a board. Drill a shallow hole in each square, and then cut pieces of twigs to fit into the holes. Color the top of some pieces black and leave the others natural. Keep the set in a baggie so you don't lose the pieces, and you'll be ready to play wherever you are.

Magnets

This project will take you just minutes to finish. Cut slices of any seasoned dry wood and sand them smooth. Glue a good magnet on the back. Then, woodburn a design or words and, if desired, color it with permanent markers. If you make your slices from dry, seasoned branches, you won't end up with checking, splitting, or bark that peels off or loosens from the wood.

 The carbon footprint of your Swiss Army Knife is similar to that of your toast at breakfast.

Napkin Rings

Stick a nice cloth napkin into one of these rings to bring an extra touch of class to the dinner table. These sleek napkin rings will turn your next meal into a memorable event, whatever the dish! There's really no rule on how thick to make the slices, but I'd aim at something close to ¾" (19mm).

Index Note: Page numbers in italics indicate projects.

alligator, *70–73*
animals, branch
  about: ideal wood
    fork, 65; overview of
    projects, 64
  alligator, *70–73*
  back scratcher, *77*
  bird, *78–81*
  dog, *77*
  donkey, *77*
  goat, *77*
  horse pen, *74–76*
  owl, *66–69*
  pen options, *74–77*
arrow and bow, *55–57*
back scratcher, *77*
bases, 105
bevel of blade, 83
bird, *78–81*
blade, bevel of, 83
blade, tapering point, 13
boats, *58–63*
bow and arrow, *55–57*
branches. *See* wood
brushes, paint, 22
carving tools, other, 23
checkers, *131*
chick, *104*
cleaning and oiling knives,
  30
cloth, for catching chips,
  22
coasters, *130*
crochet hook, *42–44*
crocodile, 73. *See also*
  alligator
curl creations
  about: bases for, 105;
    blade bevel for, 83;
    carving curls, 84–85;
    overview of projects,
    82; wet vs. dry wood
    for, 83
  chick, *104*
  flower, *86–88*
  hen, *102–3*
  heron, *106–10*
  pheasant, *101*
  roadrunner, *111–17*
  rooster, *92–101*
  squirrel, *118–25*
  tree, *89–91*
cutting strokes
  carving curls, 84–85
  drawcutting, 19
  safety tips, 18
  straightaway cutting, 19
  thumbpushing, 19
  V-notch, 19
dieter's tasting spoons, *49*
difficulty of projects, 24
dog, *77*
donkey, *77*
drawcutting, 19
fabric, for catching chips,
  22
finishes, 23, 24, 31
flower, *86–88*

fork, *35–37*
fork, ideal wood, 65
freshness, of wood, 21
gloves, 18
glues, 22
goat, *77*
grain, of wood, 20, 65
handsaw, 23
hen, *102–3*
heron, *106–10*
Hiker knife, 14
horse pen, *74–76*
JetSetter knife, 46
jewelry. *See* necklaces;
  pendant
jewelry trees, *129*
key ring, removing, 12
keychain, *39*
knife project, *26–31*
knitting needles, *40–41*
knives. *See* Swiss Army
  Knives
magnets, *134*
markers, 22
modifying knives, 12–13
name logs, *38*
name pins/pendants,
  38–39
napkin rings, *135*
necklaces, *132*
nest, making, *102*
oiling knives, 30
owl, *66–69*
paints and brushes, 22
pencil, 22
pendant, *39*
pens, animal, *74–77*
pheasant, *101*
pith, of branch, 21, 65
poker, *33*
projects, overview of, 24
Recruit knife, 15
roadrunner, *111–17*
rooster, *92–101*
rotary tool, 23
rowboat, *63*
safety tips, 18
sailboat, *58–62*
sandpaper, 22
sap, avoiding, 21
saw (handsaw), 23
sharpening and honing,
  16–17
  bevel of blade, 83
  importance of, 10, 16
  step-by-step, illustrated,
    17
  tools for, 16
simple, stunning projects.
  See also slices
  about: overview of, 126
  table art, *128*
  utensil and jewelry trees,
    129
slices
  checkers, *131*
  coasters, *130*
  magnets, *134*

napkin rings, *135*
necklaces, *132*
tic tac toe, *133*
spoons, *45–48, 49*
spreader, *32*
squirrel, *118–25*
straightaway cutting, 19
supplies and tools, 22–23.
  See also Swiss Army
  Knives
Swiss Army Knives
  choosing, 12, 14–15
  cleaning and oiling, 30
  Hiker, 14
  ideal blade bevel, 83
  JetSetter, 46
  lifetime warranty, 15
  modifying, 12–13
  Recruit, 15
  removing key ring, 12
  sharpening. *See*
    sharpening and honing
  smallest, about, 15
  tapering blade point, 13
  Tinker, 13, 14
Swiss Army Knives (facts
  and anecdotes)
  for Boy Scouts, 72
  carbon footprint of, 134
  concert piano repair
    with, 67
  emblem trademark, 112
  history of, 104, 110,
    112, 116
  for kids, first one, 53
  life-saving episodes, 85,
    93, 95
  Museum of Modern Art
    (MOMA) collection, 56
  office tools in, 46
  orbiting Earth, 71
  "parcel carrier" hook, 43
  pocketknife history and,
    98, 103
  range of worldwide
    uses, 71
  recycling practices,
    23, 37
  reputation/legacy, 59
  steel used, 23, 28
  styles of knives, 13
  train repair with, 79
  Victorinox name origin,
    116
  Victorinox products
    besides, 120
  warranty, 15
  watch recovered from
    ocean, 90

towel, for catching chips,
  22
toys
  about: overview of
    projects, 50–51
  bow and arrow, *55–57*
  rowboat, *63*
  sailboat, *58–62*
  Whimmy Diddle, *52–54*
tree, *89–91*
trees, utensil/jewelry, *129*
utensil and jewelry trees,
  129
utensils and tools, easy
  projects
  about: finishing, 24;
    overview of projects,
    24–25
  crochet hook, *42–44*
  dieter's tasting spoons,
    49
  fork, *35–37*
  keychain, *39*
  knife, *26–31*
  knitting needles, *40–41*
  name logs, *38*
  name pins/pendants, *38*
  pendant, *39*
  poker, *33*
  spoons, *45–48, 49*
  spreader, *32*
  whisk, *34*
Victorinox name origin,
  116
Victorinox products, other,
  120
V-notch, 19
washing branches, 21
Whimmy Diddle, *52–54*
whisk, *34*
whittling
  catching chips in cloth,
    22
  knives for. *See* Swiss
    Army Knives
  safety tips, 18
  sharpness of knife
    and, 10, 16. *See also*
    sharpening and honing
  wearing gloves while, 18
wood
  blanks, assorted, 20
  branches, characteristics
    of, 20–21
  fork, ideal, 65
  freshness of, 21
  grain, 20, 65
  pith size, 21, 65
  sap, avoiding, 21
  washing branches, 21
  wet vs. dry, for curls, 83
woodburner, 22
woodcarving tools, other,
  23